6 Years in the MIDDLE EAST

6Years *in the* MIDDLE EAST

A PICTORIAL JOURNEY, 2003–2009

T E N A C I T Y

SIX YEARS IN THE MIDDLE EAST
A PICTORIAL JOURNEY, 2003–2009

iUniverse books may be ordered through booksellers or by contacting:

iUniverse LLC
1663 Liberty Drive
Bloomington, IN 47403
www.iuniverse.com
1-800-Authors (1-800-288-4677)

ISBN: 978-1-4917-4681-3 (sc)
ISBN: 978-1-4917-4682-0 (hc)
ISBN: 978-1-4917-4680-6 (e)

Library of Congress Control Number: 2014917822

Printed in the United States of America.

iUniverse rev. date: 10/03/2014

This is the story of a Department of Defense contractor who served with the military in Qatar, Iraq, Kuwait, Afghanistan, and Oman. It's also a love story, which just happened along the way.

For my dad, Bob, who served with shoes on the sand in North Africa and then marched up the boot of Italy from Salerno to Mount Casino. I also give a special mention to Clio, the muse of history.

Preface

I was at a gathering of veterans in 2003, and there was an exceptional veteran there who learned that I had diabetes, which resulted in my ischemic heart. No one in my family is diabetic, but I'd had ketoacidosis and had almost died when doctors drained liters of a black substance from my abdomen a decade before. For six weeks I was in intensive care, living off nutrients injected into my blood. I was unable to drink water, let alone eat. The veteran told me the cause was Agent Orange and that the Veterans Affairs Department would cover me since I had served in Vietnam and especially because I flew in Hueys in the area where most of the Agent Orange had been released for defoliation.

My three children were grown and finally off to college or full-time work. It was time for a change from my Mr. Mom life, so I applied for many jobs online, from Antarctica to Iraq. Fortunately, I came in second for the Antarctica gig. The South Pole mission contracted something like bird flu, which spread through some ineffective carbon filters of the attached buildings. Fifteen percent of the people died, while the survivors received a Medevac out when winter subsided. Hardly a soul could walk. That was a real close call for me.

The Iraq job happened very quickly afterward. A company called SK called me, and I had an interview over the phone. I was flown out to Washington, DC; had an hour-and-a-half-long interview; and was hired on the condition I could obtain a Department of Defense (DoD) card, secret clearance, and a valid passport. I did, and in a couple of weeks, I was off to Iraq and to spend six years in the Middle East.

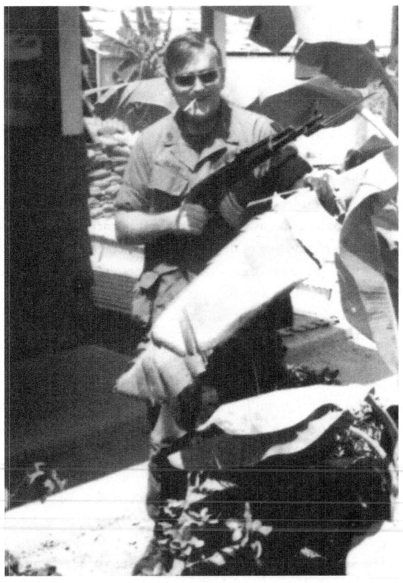

The only picture I have of me in Vietnam, at
Red Beach, North of Da Nang 1971.

Iraq, 2003

When the Iraq War broke out in the spring of 2003, no one knew what was going on, and there were no real systems in place. I had my Department of Defense (DoD) travel orders, but no destination had been specified beyond "Saddam's palace in Baghdad." In 2003, few contractors traveled by themselves, and there was no established process. We didn't go through any training and were not even given an exam. Everything we did was at our own risk. The only real bonus the government gave us back then was to waive our taxes if we stayed a full year. I was excited at the prospect of experiencing an adventure once again in a foreign land.

It took several days to get there. London was nice but very expensive. A McDonald's fish sandwich, fries, and a small Coke was more than eight dollars. I ate with a French-speaking kid, a twenty-three-year-old from New Caledonia, an island northeast of Australia. He was going to college in Lyon and studying ecology so he could protect his island home from pollution. The local people were fascinating to watch, and they plodded through their banal existence at Heathrow Airport. We had a three-hour layover before we took off for Bahrain and then Doha, Qatar. An older lady, a former hippy with hand-painted jeans, was on the Bahrain flight, and she put up the two armrests, stretched out, and slept for the whole flight (the only smart person aboard). I sat across the aisle from a Briton who had been on the Olympics water polo and swim teams of 1972. The Hungarians knocked them out early, so his four years of preparation went down the drain. He got off in Bahrain, and I had an hour layover as the plane refueled. I began to anticipate the climate and the people. I knew my life was changing for the positive, and it felt good.

Qatar

I got to Doha at 9:00 p.m., got through customs, got all my luggage, and obtained a visa that let me spend three weeks in Iraq. There was no one there from DoD. I was in an Arab nation and had no help. The hotels in Doha were all full, and neither my phone card nor my debit card worked. My DoD orders said I was to report to Al Udeid Air Base. I asked a couple of American contractors where it was; they didn't know but said a cabbie would. I asked a cabbie and showed him the paper so pronunciation wouldn't be a factor. He talked to the other cabbies and then said okay. I was fifteen minutes away from the airport when I realized that he spoke no English (other than "okay") and was not from Doha but Cairo, Egypt. He didn't know the area and was just as lost as I was. I told him to stop and ask for directions, and I got out for support. We got directions and opinions from sixteen different people. We arrived at Al Udeid sixty minutes later, after what should have been a twenty-minute ride, and the cabbie charged me forty dollars rather than the usual twenty-dollar fee. I didn't care, because I didn't know what normal was. He left me five miles or so from the base, so I hitched a ride.

A car with two people—an Arab from Doha and an American lieutenant colonel from Reno, Nevada—stopped to pick me up. They were security people at Al Udeid, and were amazed when they heard to which neighborhoods I'd been. I told them my cabbie spoke Farsi, and I watched for emotion. In my opinion, I'd never been at risk. They took a shine to me and drove me to a place where I got a pillow, sheets, and a blanket. They then showed me where I would sleep; I stored my baggage, and they took me to the mess hall. It was real hot (more than 100 degrees), but it was a dry heat. The Quonset hut had a long, cylindrical canvas at the top with had holes in it to let out the air-conditioning. You actually needed the blanket in there. I found out my visa would cost sixty dollars a day if I didn't get an exit visa, so I talked to the security guy from Doha, and he fixed me up. The sand was everywhere and bright white. I had to get flight arrangements to Baghdad and my visa stamped, so I hitchhiked to another fort and handled things. I took a shuttle bus to Al Udeid and then hitchhiked to the fort with my luggage. Again, the soldiers were amazed that I'd hitchhiked, but I told them people would sooner pick up an idiot than an armed soldier.

At the terminal, there were soldiers crashing everywhere, some of them writhing together on the floor. I realized they were men and women dressed in fatigues and obviously several were couples. They had been on a quick R&R to Bahrain and were headed back to Iraq. The army had changed considerably since I was a soldier in 1970. I got to my flight—a C130—to Baghdad without any problems; only an FBI guy and many army infantrymen got on board with me. The C130 was the type of aircraft I'd flown in Vietnam: four engines, a drop-rear tailgate, and the loudest and bounciest ride ever. They even gave us earplugs before we got on. I landed at Baghdad International Airport (BIAP) after a three-hour ride on the indestructible C130. Of course, no one was there to meet and greet me, and once again I had to improvise.

Baghdad

I decided on the same plan I'd used in Qatar. My orders said CPA (Coalition Provisional Authority), and I knew I was staying at the palace. I dragged my luggage across a parking lot covered in rocks, so the wheels on the suitcases were worthless, and it looked like I'd just bulldozed the lot. I had to find transportation, so I talked to a captain with lots of equipment; he was the officer-in-charge (OIC) media boss for the armed forces, and I helped him get all his stuff to the bus stop. He got me on a bus that took me close to the palace in the Green Zone, and then called a vehicle (with a cute female driver) that took me right to the front door. It pays to be observant.

I hauled my burden up to the palace gates, where I was stopped. I had my DoD ID and my passport, but apparently I needed one from the CPA to enter. Again, no one knew I was coming, so I explained everything to the powers that be. Eventually they accepted my IDs and processed me into the country. It was now Tuesday, the fourteenth, around 3:00 p.m. local time (and eight hours earlier in Chicago). The processing center called my partner in Iraq, a bright twenty-three-year-old named Khalid who had grown up in Oklahoma. His dad was the CFO for an Arab embassy in Washington, DC, and his mom was the director of postgraduate studies. He would pick me up in the office on the morrow; in the meantime, they got me a cot in the north wing of the palace. I leaned back in one officer's chair, and my weight sheared off one of the five wheels; down I went. I wasn't hurt, but the guy no longer had a chair. Someone gave me sheets, a blanket, and a pillow and took me to my new quarters with three hundred other poor unfortunates. I met a good DEA guy there named Jim, who had been to Germany and volunteered for seven weeks to train the Iraq police force.

SATCOM SK Tech.

The palace was gorgeous, but a lot of it was under construction. The amount of marble alone could fill a football stadium. I opened my luggage and realized I had not packed shampoo or soap. I was exhausted, so I crashed on my cot around 8:00 p.m. and woke up when it was still dark, around 3:00 a.m. I couldn't get back to sleep, so I decided to take a shower. then walked in my socks about a half mile to the only accessible showers. It was like *M*A*S*H*; there were posted times for women in one of the two buildings, and they could use the shower for four hours at two different times. I dressed in a polo shirt and wash pants and walked back to the eating area; breakfast was from 6:30 a.m. to 8:30 a.m. On the way, I adjusted my load and apparently dropped my DoD ID and my sixty-minute phone card (the one that had not worked in Doha). I sat with Gurkhas (guards from Nepal and ate with them around 5:00 a.m. They must have thought I was an advisor or something, because no one stopped me. I reported my lost ID, which I'd obtained at the Great Lakes naval base, and sure enough the nearest place to replace it was Kuwait. This prompted the staff to hurry up and process my in-country card. The staff was all cute Hungarian girls, who I teased unmercifully.

After I got the in-country card, Khalid and I went to the ministry of industry. It was like a video game to get there, driving zigzag around concrete blocks—at five miles per hour because if we drove faster, spikes would pierce our tires—through checkpoints with armed guards, and past M-1 tanks and Bradley's everywhere. The ministry was called Ground Zero because it contained the provisional Iraq government and their electable future. They were drawing up their constitution (ours took eleven years), so Ground Zero was the main terrorist-threatened spot in Iraq. There were five explosions at a nearby gate as we arrived, but no one I knew was hurt. Twenty-some people were dead, all Iraqi.

I met the staff (mostly Iraqi) and was part of the team whose mission was to get a phone breakthrough by applying our technology to their land lines, which we'd cut in the first Iraq War. We were trying to get Western parts to work with Eastern protocols, and it was a nightmare.

I used my first Eastern toilet, which were two different holes in the ground. One was six inches across for urinating, and the other was eighteen inches by sixteen inches–plus, almost teardrop shape, with serrated edges in porcelain protruding four inches from each side of the aperture. You'd squat over the hole, and the ridges would keep your feet from sliding.

My size-thirteen shoe on the toilet.

After a long day—an 8:30 a.m. start until a 9:00 p.m. stop—Khalid took me back to the converted palace ballroom with400 cots. I was determined to stay up longer, and since I still had neither soap nor shampoo, I decided to go to Saddam's palace pool. It had plenty of chlorine and burned my eyes and crotch, but I felt like it was cleaning me too. The pool was huge, with a one-meter board and a three-meter platform. There was a huge fountain on one side and tile everywhere. It was very deep everywhere but on one side, and the tile was so slippery on the bottom, I couldn't stand up. It was truly Saddam's pool, because wherever I was in the pool I was over my head; and if not, it was slippery ground. I measured the pool at forty-five-plus yards long and about twenty yards wide.

A great cooling-off spot at the palace.

I tried to sleep late, but I woke up at 5:00 a.m. and talked to Jim, the DEA agent, at breakfast. I met Khalid at 8:30 a.m, and off we went through the video game. Someone had found my DoD ID, so we were to pick it up on our way back. And the satellite manager had the key to a trailer for me.

We had a nice lunch (lamb, chicken, rice, and an Iraqi sweet dessert, ladyfingers, which looked like light-beige eggrolls). An Iraqi man next to me bit into one and sprayed my good light-blue shirt. I bought some body wash at the hotel for five dollars, and we went back to the palace around 8:00 p.m. and picked up my card, duffle bags and the trailer key. The trailer was great; there were four people to a unit (two bedrooms) with a common shower, toilet, and sink. I had a bed, a small locking closet, and an end table with a desk lamp. At first, I did not have a roommate, so it was doubly nice. I slept till almost 7:00 a.m. on Friday and had a nice body-wash shower and breakfast. Friday was like our Sunday; no one went to work, except security. I wanted to go to the airport for supplies and drive the gauntlet through the non-secured area called the Red Zone. Khalid agreed to go with me—he liked to drive fast too—so I began the videogame course, zigzagged past the obstacles and guard stations, and got out straightaway. The five-speed Hyundai could not go very fast, but it was fun. I was zipping along at 130 to 150 kilometers per hour (80 to 93 miles per hour), which was pretty fast for town. I had to slow down quickly at blockades and tanks, because the military were wary of speeding civilian vehicles, which could have been suicide bombers, but I had a blast. I got to the Base Exchange at the airport and bought sneakers, shampoo, a prayer rug for a bath mat, watch, laundry bag, pretzels and a special holder for my ID badge. I told the Iraqi who sold the prayer rug to me that it was for the bath, and he was miffed; so I told him my cultural group prays wet. I drove the gauntlet back, and it was great with the weather, wind, and videogame atmosphere. I felt like I was making progress, especially after I took all my travel clothes to the laundry.

*With his five heads looking down at you, there
was no doubt whose palace it had been.*

We had a little rain the next morning, for five minutes while I was walking to breakfast. When Khalid got up forty-five minutes later it was all dry, and he thought I was lying to him. I had breakfast at the palace with a cute woman from Arlington, Virginia, but I think she thought I was a little crazy. She was trying to find political power and add some consideration to her resume. Many of the staff and officers were just getting career enhancements. They rarely left the palace or billet area and were only in country for a couple of months. Saturday there was like our Saturday—a half day of work for the locals, who had taken a full day off on Friday.

My eyes are hazel, my hair is light-brown peppered with gray, and I usually sport a goatee. I have very fair skin that sunburns easily so I have to be careful outside. My water consumption increased ten times. I drank more water than Diet Coke (Coca-Cola Light in Iraq), and if you know me, you know that's a lot of water. I think I was the only person there who doesn't smoke. They had hookahs, cigars, and cigarettes (Marlboro was big). When three or four smokers got together, it was terrible. I thought I would die of lung cancer. The only physical exercise I did (besides surviving) was in the pool one night. I went to the gym, which was pretty nice, considering where we were. I screwed up and didn't shoot up with insulin before I left home, so I knew not to have anything but water and exercise. Wearing a bathing suit and undershirt, I did some free weights and hit the bike for a half hour. I was overweight and in my late fifties, but you have to keep in condition when you're in a hostile environment. (A few nights later, I saw a skinny slip of a girl working out; I was impressed by how many real pushups she could do.) I walked over to Saddam's pool; there were lots of people there, but no one was swimming. Some were watching college football, which aired around 8:00 p.m. on Saturdays; others were just talking. Unabashed, I went swimming, and wouldn't you know—like a junior high dance—as soon as I was in the pool, several more got in as well. (Apparently, no one wanted to be the first.)

Political correctness abounds; when boiled, beef bacon looks purple

Sunday was a big workday; Sunday to Thursday is the Iraqi workweek. I was in the line for breakfast with a charming chap with a white beard; he looked like a shah. He turned out to be the UN chief of humanitarian affairs and a teacher from Liverpool, England (the Beatles' hometown). He was very concerned about the police situation, and I told him it would take five years to get a handle on it. He agreed, and we chatted for a half-hour. He offered his cell phone, and I called Dad to see how the new house was working out, forgetting that it was midnight back in North Carolina. I had applied for a phone but didn't have one yet. I feared I'd have to take action because normal channels didn't seem to work.

I finally met the guy on the other side of the trailer. He was the deputy director for private sector development and was from Poland. I told him I was from the second-largest Polish city in the world: Chicago. He liked that, and I said, "Dubcha." I don't know what it means, but it always makes Polish people laugh.

We downloaded videos from the Internet; apparently people go to the movies with video cameras; they recorded the flick and then converted it to AVI format so we could watch it on our PCs. It took me about twenty-four hours to download half of a two-hour movie. The bandwidth of the sender and receiver made a big difference.

Everything in Baghdad was white sand and dust, and it was difficult to keep shoes clean. I bought some New Balance sneakers at the PX, but even though they were size 13D, they seemed tight. Maybe my feet grew? I picked up my laundry one morning, and it was wrinkled beyond belief. My attempt to speak Arabic was a total disaster, and no one understood my accent. Apparently, just as French has its rolling R, Arabic has letters that you have to learn to project correctly. It is a very guttural yet sing-song-sounding language.

I went to lunch at the Al Rasheed Hotel, and after I filled my tray full, I went looking for Khalid so we could sit together. I wasn't paying attention and walked into a floor pool. Fortunately, there was no water. The staff tried to help, but it made things worse, and I lost my entire lunch. My fries, peas, and carrots went all over the place, so I considered it a sign from God and got two apples instead. When we returned to the Ministry of Industry, we took the videogame route through the blockades and then stopped at a gate (like the ones they have in Europe at the borders, the ones with the long, striped poles). The guard looked at our IDs and then took a mirror on a pole to look under our vehicle for bombs. The gate came up and the tire slashers went down, and we drove toward a "saw" (a type of machine gun) that was aimed at the windshield.

Gurkhas are fierce and well trained: stop and be recognized, or die.

A new guy came in, and I let him stay with me but that made it more crowded. I didn't know when he would leave, but he was from SK headquarters and, according to him, was going to solve all our problems. I introduced him as the company troubleshooter who would take care of everyone's grievances, and he smiled and agreed. (I'm such a little stinker.) The best the guy could do now was take care of all the problems, and of course he would get the heat for all the ones he couldn't fix.

I went for a trim and shave. It was both exciting and interesting to have an Iraqi put a razor against my neck. My ride had left, so I walked the mile back to work on the Red Zone border. The Americans think I'm crazy, but no one bothered an unarmed, walking, bearded man. I had no Kevlar on my chest or a helmet to draw attention. It was a beautiful day in the upper 80s and, of course, very dry. At a good-bye party for someone who was leaving, people voted to keep me in Baghdad because they all liked my laugh. No one seemed to care about my education or computer skills.

On Friday—again, there were no Iraqis to speak of—we went to the BX (base exchange) at the airport. I couldn't believe the duty-free prices. All the guys—there were four others besides Khalid and me—wanted to get booze. A quart of good vodka was seven dollars. I got a box of M&M's with four small bags of peanut and four small bags of regular, and it cost six dollars. I felt like I was being punished for not being an alcoholic. I bought a digital camera and learned to use it and download files to e-mail home.

Captain M, my boss, and Major X, security.

I needed a permit to carry a personal weapon, so I got in touch with Major X, and he obtained the cards I needed to carry weapons, whether concealed or not. Interestingly, I could not get a gun from the CPA in Baghdad, but I could buy one in the Red Zone. I picked up an old .45, like the one I had in Vietnam, for road trips. But the US army did not have any ammo for it; they only had 9 mm rounds. I had to get my rounds at the Italian camp, whose officers still used the Colt 1911. I didn't plan on shooting anyone, and I had no confidence in a 9 mm providing protection, only in its ability to maim people. The .45 would stop a car or truck, and that's all I'd ever need to do (I hoped). Most roadside attacks involved two vehicles trying to force you off the road, so the .45 would end that drama. If I never had to use it, that would be even better. I never wore it so it was visible.

I kept this Colt 1911 in my backpack, just in case.

Another manager moved into my trailer, so I had Robert (who is now sick), Tim (who took a truck to Al Hillah and left all his stuff in my room), and Rene (who is in California had left his also). I used to have no roommates, and now I had two too many.

Driving was fun. There were no traffic laws, and lanes didn't exist. The army tried to enforce speeding regulations, but they usually just issued warnings. Only the spikes and speed bumps really worked. Khalid was the right guy to drive with, as he knew the area and spoke Arabic. He usually asked me to go with him when shipments came into the airport. Hospitality was a matter of pride and honor. The girls gave me goodies; I told them sugar was bad for me, but they were so persistent and didn't want to offend. So I'd eat their offerings—dates and nuts wrapped in some kind of nougat or sugar batter.

One day, the full bird (colonel) came to check on everything because a three-star general was to visit us the next day. I drew up a network diagram, but I was having trouble getting it plotted. Most of the army personnel were only familiar with their own software, but I found a sergeant who was on the ball, and she said she would help me. I put *Rundown* (a then-new movie starring the Rock) on a DVD for her, so she was motivated. The general was to arrive the next day at 10:30 a.m., so I wanted to get the diagram on the wall as a visual aid for a talk on what was there and how it worked.

The plotter shed was the only game in town when it came to maps and printing large documents.

The general was delayed; we heard he was supposed to come at 11:45 a.m. I had to get aerial maps of Baghdad and tape them on the roof of the building, so they could explain the city to the general from there.

I was invited to a lamb kabob/roast chicken party that night with the army brass. Khalid was to deliver the party food, but I did not go. We had a sick boss, Robert, who trashed my toilet and soaked the bathroom floor. I went to the office and found the Al Rasheed had been hit, and fifteen people were wounded. A convoy was also hit, and several contractors died. It reinforced my nonaggression view. Ramadan started that night, and I think they knew a three-star general was coming, so hitting the hotel with several rockets made sense. I went to the billeting office, where they thought I was still in the pit, and asked for accommodations at the Al Rasheed. I told them I worked across the street and that I figured after the attack they might have some openings. They said they were closing the hotel; because of the military personnel and contractors there, it was a target. I still wanted a room, and they said it was a bloody mess. I volunteered to clean it up, but was sent away. The whole area was a mess.

This is my first office in the Baghdad GOIC.

In the morning, I dropped Khalid at the GOIC (Governing Office of the Intermediate Counsel), which was where we worked, and returned to pick up Charles, Robert, and Eric and to see if the plotting room was open. (It wasn't.) There wouldn't be any cute network pictures for the general, but at least I had the older test to put up. I had grand fun driving by myself, and I made it to the palace without incident. I dropped the three guys at the forum, which was between the GOIC and the Al Rasheed, so they could check on the phones. Five more bombs went off; they intended to bring in the holiday with a bang. I went to the roof and taped some aerial photos to a couple of desks. The Green Zone had been drawn on them, so I angled the photo to ensure it matched the actual view and placed a giant rivet to indicate where we were. Ed, who is an Iraqi and has a PhD, was going to give the presentation to the general, showing him the classroom, server room, and the roof view of the city. Major G was to fill in where necessary. But the walkthrough was delayed because of the new bombs. I was sure we were all over the news, but it was nothing compared to Vietnam and the physical concussions caused by large explosions or napalm. In Baghdad, small arms fire was limited; most of the attacks were bombs and rockets. Our head of security lived at the Al Rasheed, and he said he was moving out. I hoped they would at least still serve lunch there. I didn't want to have to go back to the palace for lunch. It was a zoo there, with way too many people at that point.

A Gurkha guarding the palace with a khukuri knife.

The three-star general arrived. He shook my hand, and we had lunch with a dozen others. General S is the head of J-6, which is the Signal Corps and includes computers and satellite dishes. When the general's staff asked Ed about his politics, he said he had none and had lived in Baghdad for the last year and a half. He'd received a scholarship to India and $65 a month. The Iraqi government would not let him go because he wasn't a member of the Ba'ath party, so he signed up. They gave him no other assistance—Ba'ath scholarships were more than $1,200 a month for regular party members, even those with poor grades—but he graduated after five years. The general's staff was impressed and seemed as though they wanted him to run for the presidency. Ed explained his education had helped remove his emotional involvement in politics. When asked about "terrorists," he said they were mostly Ba'ath party members who had no skills, so they were crying out because they'd had everything before the war and now they had nothing. I almost felt sorry for the terrorists. The staff then asked about the average education level among Iraqis, and Ed said, "high school." When they asked him why the Iraqis didn't have his attitude, Ed seemed confused, so I chimed in and said, "Most Iraqis haven't had Ed's cosmopolitan viewpoint and education. They have not traveled more than twenty-five miles from their homes and have a high-school education or less." He seemed relieved and agreed with my response.

General S was the head of the Signal Corps.

I respected this general, as did his men. He was the only ranking individual who used his own soldiers for security in the Red Zone. Most of the others had Blackwater mercenaries or helicopters. General S drove to the GOIC, and his guys were all Signal Corps troops.

We had to complete another project and that was to call the United States—specifically area code 914 in New York—without using our cellular system. Iraq was not connected directly, so we used a phone card in Arabic. The first Iraqi international phone call, using Chinese E1 exchange cards, was to my son, Bob, in Joliet, Illinois. He picked up the historic call, while the staff, general, and several officers listened. (Captain M, our DoD client, was very pleased.) We conducted the walkthrough on the next two floors, planning data and phone for each room. We planned to be completely wired before Christmas, but there was always the unexpected.

After the entourage left, I took Ed in front of the other Iraqis and said, "Ed for president." Then I took out a tissue, wiped his mouth, and told him I had to clean his lips since he'd kissed the general's butt. Everyone laughed. I then presented him with a pack of Wrigley's spearmint gum and told him that after his presentation, he was now a member of the Order of Black Arrow (the gum pack has arrow on the front). I found these people to be kind, generous, and full of good humor, very different from what was shown on the news. Most were looking for a better life and were relieved to have no more oppression from Saddam. I believed, as Ed did, that education and a generation of change was required to heal and get Iraqis to be fully productive members of the global community. Ed said, "If you take down a tyrant and don't educate, another will take his place, and the book will go back to the beginning again."

We returned to the palace that night after a hectic day of attacks, and I watched the Dallas/Tampa Bay game (a 9:00 p.m. start there) by Saddam's pool. Wouldn't you know it, some Ba'ath guys set off some rockets, and they turned off the game and ordered everyone into the palace. I don't think I got to see fifteen minutes of it. The following Monday morning, Robert was still sick in my room. Our power had been out since the general was there for lunch. Our PCs and the satellite and server worked because of battery backup and a diesel generator. But all the lights were off, and the building had a weird glow caused by the PC screens. Three more bombs went off; Ramadan in Iraq was kind of like Tet, the New Year's holiday in Vietnam, when the activity of subversives increased dramatically.

An M-19 grenade launcher will make things messy very quickly.

We had only one vehicle, and everyone wanted to use it for various reasons. I stayed out of the political struggle. I now had at least four bosses. Testosterone was everywhere. Everyone claimed to have a powerful friend at the home office. I couldn't play the game because I didn't know (or care about) the pecking order. I'd spent all of two hours at the home office in Washington, DC, and I knew my boss (and knew about his boss), two HR people, and one secretary.

The rockets that pelted the hotel were launched from a fake generator. It had been set up, pulled by a truck and then elevated. It was actually quite close to the hotel and looked innocent enough. The entire attack was remote, and there was no chance the perpetrators would be caught. After the attacks, only half of the workers showed up. Ten people were killed at the Red Cross, a mile away from the palace, during a car bombing. The count reached thirty-nine, with twelve total at the Red Cross, and the rest were Iraqi policemen. At 9:00 p.m. on Monday night, some Iraqi policemen ran around with some Ba'ath party members, trying to start something in the Green Zone. Ramadan brought out the worst in the bad guys I guess. It definitely was not dull there.

A generator similar to this one was used to attack Al Rasheed Hotel.

Robert kept me up half the night with his phone calls and by keeping his light on till 1:30 a.m. At 4:15 a.m., he got up and went to pray (it was Ramadan) and had breakfast before the sun rose. He'd get back at 5:30 a.m., but one day he left his phone plugged in, and it rang twenty times during the hour and a half he was gone. He then would go to sleep, and I'd rise around 6:15 a.m. to shower. He kept the room key and could nap at intervals all day.

He still had a sore throat, so I cut him some slack. I am the only Indian with all the Chiefs here. Everyone claimed to be my boss. It was great to support such a fine group of managers all by myself.

When I was on the phone with my mother, we were hit by rockets flying over the palace. One shook the trailer pretty good, but I didn't know if anyone had been hurt. I took pictures of the Al Rasheed attack, but I couldn't get upstairs to show the interior damage (there was too much blood). The place was evacuated, and only a couple of stores remained open. As it turned out, a bird colonel (one of ours) had been eliminated. Again, a wooden cart had been made to look like a portable generator. There were four snipers on top of the Rasheed with infrared and light-gathering scopes, and no one was able to identify the perp. Apparently, our Blackwater guys are easily duped. Fortunately some of the ordinances didn't go off, or the casualties would have been much higher.

Pounded by rockets hidden in a fake generator.

A Reporter's Questions

In the fall of 2003, I received some questions from a reporter in the eastern United States. Her questions and my answers are reproduced below.

Question:
As I understand it, your job is to head up the task of rebuilding the computer network in Baghdad. Is that correct? What kind of shape are things in? What were your first thoughts? What will be your first or your biggest challenge? Does the task seem more foreboding than you might have imagined, or less foreboding, or about what you expected?

Answer:
Specifically, I am in the building that houses the provisional government of Iraq while they create their new constitution. We have three floors done and were just awarded a contract for the next three. We provide the network capability to two buildings (GOIC and the "White House"). Currently, the next three floors are being specified as to furniture and carpet (this is very important for face). I really am not rebuilding all of Baghdad, but I am rebuilding a network for the new government. A lot of the floors were shot up, not by the bombing, but by the occupying troops that were bored or disgruntled after the occupation of Baghdad. (I've been told

this by locals but [have] not witnessed [it].) We have old Asian custom circuits and central phone offices that are terrible by US standards; the main electric[ity] was installed when I was born (1947). But I feel it's getting better, and we have about 20 percent of a Western … phone structure in Baghdad.

I have no thoughts on my biggest challenge other than [to gain] the trust of the people here. Americans and other nationals forget we are the invaders, and this is their country. Would we be happy with Russians telling us what to do? As to foreboding, I never felt it at all. I view it as an opportunity to do some good and change some Third World opinion[s] about us. To the Arab mind-set, we are quite rude in our directness and efficiency. They are collective and venture out with group opinions only, unless [it is a] secret.

We worked for the secretary general and the twenty-five delegates of the governing council.

Question:

What are your impressions of the temperament of the people? As far as what you see and hear, what do most Iraqis think [about] Americans and their efforts? What do they [the Iraqis] think about the civilian violence of the last few weeks?

Answer:

The temperament of the people I come in contact [with] is docile and respectful (at work) and fearful (during explosions). Like all civilians, they are interested in their own survival and what they can do to make a living. They are friendly and want to please, and I don't employ or command any aspect of their lives. I have not met any inner Ba'ath party members—just one who was forced to join to get his scholarship—and I haven't got a chance to meet any Shiites (mostly [from cities in] southern Iraq, like Basra). I did meet a nice Kurdish girl who was educated in Great Britain. Her uncle is on the interim governing council here, and she has a British husband in Canada. Most of the people here are from Baghdad [where they've spent] their whole lives. They say the violence is terrible, and that most Muslims are not like that, and it is against Muhammad's teaching and the Koran. I don't think they love the Americans here, but they don't want to go back to what they had. Some want the Americans to rule; others want us out immediately; and still others like the idea of a slow turnover. They like the fact the Americans are rebuilding the infrastructure but also feel we destroyed it.

Question:

From what you see and hear, in what kind of shape is the morale of the American military and other Americans there? Do you have any observations that hit you as different about the situation in

Iraq from what you had heard stateside or from what the media in general is reporting?

Answer:

The American soldiers [have] mixed … feelings; some [are] even bored. Some have been caught sleeping on guard duty, which is a super no-no. Most troops I see are fairly positive, but they are volunteer soldiers and, for the most part, would rather be at home. There are many women soldiers here and, like Jessica Lynch, [they] are in harm's way. They all have the normal grumblings of an army, but the called-up reserves are probably the most unhappy (because they really didn't sign up for this). The highest morale would probably be [among] the officers in the palace. We get lots of intelligence reports here. For example, tonight [Wednesday, October 29], we heard that one hundred "mad" bombers were going to attack during a sandstorm. We are having a sandstorm, and everyone is [really] concerned. One of our guys wants to get out of country; he left early to go to the palace. Others want to get guns (like we need more paranoid people with guns), and people are getting serious looks on their faces. The CNN for the United States is different than the CNN for the Middle East. The death tolls and contractor deaths [listed] are different on each.

Question:

With the bombing of the Al Rasheed Hotel and the five car bombings over the weekend, both in your first couple of weeks in Baghdad, have you had concerns for your personal safety? Does your Vietnam experience prove valuable?

Answer:

Concerns for my personal safety, I'll leave to God, luck, or fate. In dangerous combat, you only live in the present and react accordingly. I feel Vietnam was helpful in the sense [that] I know how bad it can get and that even the best planning won't always save you. [A positive] attitude will keep you mentally healthy and focused. For me, humor and viewpoint rule the day and will even save or motivate others.

Blood Days

It was 5:30 a.m. on Thursday, October, 30, and all the carrying on about the one hundred mad bombers had dwindled away. My group had elected to stay at the GOIC, but I couldn't really sleep on the hard floor or in a chair that well. One of the guys was going through a quitting tirade with the guy who had hired me. I wished him well and hope he won his individual work stoppage. If he didn't get satisfaction soon, we'd be taking him to the airport later that day. I didn't hear any bombs, but there was been a sandstorm with high winds most of the night. Intel then said the one-hundred-man suicide attack was on for the next seventy-two hours. Khalid and Charles slept on the floor and were sawing wood pretty loudly. I could hear the Iraqis arriving for work, and I'd been up for more than twenty-five hours. All the paranoia was gone, and the bustling of the daily work had begun.

The previous night, a woman from the consulate told me that the government abandoned you in these times, and she was quite upset. She seemed to think the sandstorm was an excellent cover for the suicide attack, and I told her about my previous experience: the Vietnamese didn't fight in bad weather. During Typhoon Hester, my officers had told me the same crap and kept me up for three days straight, but the big surprise attack never came. She said, "These are desert people and will use this storm to attack," and I responded, "No, most people in Baghdad are city folk and educated. Farm people with little education and lots of religion tend to be the bombers."

Mortars and rockets damage trailers and wound or kill their occupants.

It was the evening of Friday, October 31—Halloween—and all was well. We went to the airport, and I bought a microwave, but no popcorn was available. I hooked it up, although all the instructions were in German. I also couldn't help buying a deck of "Iraqi most wanted" playing cards, in which Saddam was the ace of spades. We were still on alert, but the next day would be Blood Day for the Iraqis. One of our men was offered $2,000 (a million dinars) to shoot Americans during the day. We were waiting to see what would happen over the next thirty or so hours. I found it interesting that they had to pay so much for warriors. If you are upset and want to fight for freedom or against oppression, money is not an issue. That told me the "problem children" were few in number, even if they were dangerous. One of the mercenaries told me they captured Americans for money. I said they were no different from criminals in the United States, who will take the loved one of a wealthy person and try to sell them back. Unemployment in Iraq was 60 percent; these people needed a life and, more important, a job and a chance for self-satisfaction. Training them, giving them a police force to protect them, and finding employment was absolutely essential for Operation Iraq Freedom. Destroying them or defending ineffectively against suicide attacks was not any answer. My heart bled for the Iraqi people, and there was no easy short-term solution.

November came quickly. It actually felt like fall. I got a new territory—to document the phone system on Visio (a graphics program), and I was not a phone person. However, I had done graphics for many years. I also received permission to cash checks for $2,500, and my company SK would back them. I couldn't imagine spending that much cash over in Iraq, but it was nice to know I had the capability.

Another mortar hit on a trailer roof.

When a mortar hit, it exploded up; rockets penetrated and then exploded. We were hit by a mortar, and fortunately most of the fragments went skyward. Some guys put sandbags on their roofs, but if a rocket hit, they'd be dead. And if it were a mortar, the roof would cave from the impact and the sandbags would pummel a sleeper.

If a mortar had hit between the trailers, six trailers would have been penetrated.

A teacher, Amal; our cleaning girl, Shams (whose name means sun); and Abu Jacob (I'd bought a hat for him with that name on it) presented me with a plate with a brass ornament—a lion's body with wings and the head of an old bearded man. We put it up on the cement wall with much effort. They took turns and banged a nail into the concrete until it stayed. I gave the teacher some Kit Kat bars and a Butterfinger, and I think she was pleased. The power went out again, but as before all our PCs were powered by a backup generator. I didn't have overhead lights so I couldn't read, but at least I had the computer.

Khalid bought a twenty-nine-inch TV, and we got the local Iraqi channel and one from Iran. It was funny to watch the Iranian station because it ran Chinese shows with Iranian subtitles. The Iraq station had soap operas (they call all shows "soaps"), comedy, lots of group dancing, musicals, and dramas. Many shows seemed to have a mixture of comedy, dancing, music, and drama. It was like *Days of Our Lives*, MTV, *The Music Man*, and *Cops*, all in one half-hour show. One show that was funny had a hidden camera, like *Candid Camera*. A hidden camera crew taped a restaurant owner serving his patrons dog food. He told people it was a restaurant for dogs and asked them where their dogs were. When they discovered he had been serving dog food, they were incensed and beat him up (much like a Jerry Springer show). He told them it was very good dog food, and he asked them, "Why didn't you bring your dog?" At the end, they forgave him when they discovered they had been filmed by the show. They had a cheerful MTV-like songfest, with children singing about God and Ramadan. It was like 1950s programming in the United States.

The SK staff all had a great dinner—I paid since I was the only one with money—at an Iraqi restaurant that served great "roasted over the fire" chicken. There was plenty of steamed rice and mixed vegetables; I didn't know the variety, but they were tasty. Spices were minimal, just pepper and salt, but the natural chicken juices gave a great flavor. We ate with our fingers, and Khalid smoked a hookah, which is called something else in Arabic. Robert was not doing well and was pretty depressed. The bombings bothered him a lot, and I wondered whether he would snap out of it. Afterward, we dropped Robert at the palace and went back to the GOIC for a couple of hours. When we got back to the palace, Charles had to work for a while, so I went to the gym. When I went to my room to change, Robert was already in bed; it was 8:30 p.m. I changed, went to the gym, and took some pictures when I worked out. When I got back, Robert was still in bed, so I read my book, *The Arab Way*, and shut off my desk light around 11:00 p.m. or so.

Robert got up at 4:00 a.m. to pray and have breakfast before the sun came up; he's Muslim, and it was Ramadan). He always turned on the overhead florescent lights and woke me up, but that morning he was very excited and started wailing because the terminal (satellite dish) was down. I asked him why he was acting like Chicken Little ("the sky is falling"), and he told me again that the dish had no power and that it was supposed to be up 99 percent of the time. I asked, "Will someone die if it's not up?" And he said the region was down. The Basra and Al Hillah dishes had just been put up; they fed our dish and only worked sporadically.

"So if someone can't do e-mail or get Internet, this is a crisis," I said.

"No, the customer expects it to be up," Robert responded.

So I said, "Then this is about saving face? Please explain it to me. I don't know why we are in crisis mode." He grew dejected and lay down in his bed.

I said, "If it is so critical, and you can't find Charles to open the shelter, we should go there, and I'll help you break in. You're an engineer and should be able to get it running again."

He said he'd had it and wanted to quit and go back to his old job in the States.

Not a half hour later Colonel K, the local big boss called, and told Robert he would break into the shelter with a crowbar. Robert woke Khalid and tried to find Charles in three of the trailers, waking up everyone except Charles. I asked why Charles was the only one with a key. No one could answer that question.

Finally I said, "If you want to find Charles, why don't you wake up the billeting officer and find out where Charles lives?"

I went to the billeting place with Khalid; it was 6:40 a.m. and the office opened at 7:00 a.m. Khalid was fasting so I told him to wait there. I went to get breakfast, since no one really wanted to break in. At 7:00 a.m., Khalid got into the billeting place, but just then Charles turned on his phone, and the crisis suddenly vanished. In the meantime, I'd had breakfast with our new customer, a marine named Captain M; I relayed the events to him, and he was fine with the dish being down. He wanted to come to the GOIC at 10:30 a.m., and Khalid was to pick him up. Khalid was tired from the ordeal, so he dropped me off at the GOIC before 7:30 a.m. and went back to his trailer to snooze until he had to pick up Capt. M. I felt the whole thing was a total waste of energy and unnecessary stress. But then what else was there to do early Sunday morning?

I took Captain M back after his meeting; it was around noon, so I went to the Al Rasheed for lunch, as it had opened for chow at least. I still enjoyed driving by myself in Baghdad. We watched *Transporter* on Khalid's TV, and it was fun to watch it again. It was a slow day, so the locals left so they could get home before dark. I was monitoring the ebb node on the satellite dish and reported the figures all weekend into an Excel spreadsheet (which was like watching paint dry). I hadn't used my networking training much, but that was okay; I would do whatever was needed. Life there was interesting every day, and if we had a slow day, that was great too.

Iraqi insurgents shot down a Chinook chopper at the airport one morning. There were thirteen dead and twenty wounded, all soldiers going on R&R in Qatar. Other than that, it was quiet. At that point, more had died after the "end of the war" than during the actual invasion. I thought to myself, *This will work against Mr. Bush, and because Saddam, Osama bin Laden and weapons of mass destruction have not been found, he hasn't a chance to be reelected in 2004 unless he can redirect attention.*

On the morning of Monday, November 3, everything was okay, except Charles had unplugged the refrigerator when he made coffee the night before. I thought I might "kill" him for such a breach of common sense. The pop, ice, water, and insulin were all warm. I hoped the day would continue to be just as uneventful.

Two rockets and three mortars had hit the previous night, and the resulting fire got most of the people moving. I went up on the roof and could see the smoke from the mortars that landed by the palace. The rockets landed at the GOIC, maybe a block away from us and two blocks from the Al Rasheed. There were no casualties, so we were "lucky." One of our employees (Tim) had a P5, full-auto, 9 mm "burp gun" with ammo. He left it in the locked car, but it could be seen it through the window. I told them we were extremely lucky no one saw it, or it would have been gone. That is just common sense, especially in a hot zone. Khalid and Tim had some heated exchanges over responsibility; I don't know who won, but it was stupid.

I picked up Captain M that morning and took him to the GOIC for a phone test, now that we had it working. He was happy, and I took him to the Al Rasheed for lunch and then back to the palace. He was our customer at that point and procured money for expansion. If he looked good, then we did too. Ours was the only Western exchange that worked with the Chinese-manufactured Iraqi system. We called Mosul, Basra, and the palace on the land line.

The goal was that eventually all of Iraq would be Westernized, and it would have a good central office system with Siemens or Lucent technology. But at that point, it was really bad. We custom fit the Siemens to a Panasonic, and then to the Iraq system central office. We got the expansion contract and were to do the rest of the building. The company billed Khalid and me out at ten times our salaries, so it was in good shape. I campaigned for an increase in hostile fire pay for everyone, because of the amount and intensity of the attacks, although I wasn't sure it would do any good. I had to put in an audio-recording system for the interim government; it consisted of twenty-five microphones, recording equipment, speakers, and a computer with software so they could keep track as they created the new constitution.

I was quite proud that our system worked, even though my contribution to the technical side was minimal, and that the Iraqis did most of it themselves. The next day we were to test phone cards for international calls; by the following year, I hoped to have Iraqis with the rest of the world, dialing direct. People could call their friends and family, and they could call back. We had finished thirty full-time trunk lines and hoped to have ninety by the end of the next week as we populate the Panasonic with additional e1 cards. (E1 is used Europe; t1 is used in the United States.)

We got hit that night while I was riding the bike at the gym. All the army guys ran wildly in a scramble to get out. I didn't have a destination in mind, so I kept pedaling my bike. A man stopped the army guys at the door of the gym and said they should stay in the building. They came back, and I looked like the smart one, but it was a total accident. I finished riding and talked to an E-7 who was getting out in a year and wanted to become a computer guy. I explained which certifications and clearances he needed to get. The guards said there were two casualties by the hospital, but I couldn't confirm that.

This next morning was the walkthrough for the expansion at the GOIC. In the afternoon, we had a personal project—putting up a dish to receive satellite transmissions for our new television. Everything was made in Taiwan, so I didn't know how it would work. When I was little, everything cheap was made in Japan and was stamped as useless. Today the Japanese build many things that have higher quality than the American, so who knows about Taiwan?

I ate at the Al Rasheed once or twice a day. I thought reporters were staying there, so I wanted to try to get in, if they would let me. The hotel got shot at a lot, but it was conveniently close to work, and the food was much better there than at the palace cafeteria. To be politically correct, the Americans used beef bacon and boiled it. It was purple and awful. I was surprised we didn't have to use prayer rugs and face the East to coexist with our Iraqi partners.

This picture was printed in Hendersonville, North Carolina, and LaSalle, Illinois, newspapers in 2003.

I developed a sandbag theory based on my Vietnam experience. A mortar had exploded next to me while I was sleeping in Vietnam, but it only blew the roof off, because there were sandbags higher than the cots around my hooch. In Iraq, one mortar could take out five to nine trailers, which would be four men per trailer. The thin walls would only add to the shrapnel. I told them for $10,000—sand was plentiful there—they could get some bags and hire Iraqi workers to build them up around each trailer to protect the occupants. That would have cut the casualty rate by

90 percent if a mortar landed there. I think I got some interest at command, billeting, and grunt (guards around the palace) levels. It was an easy, preventive measure that could save a lot of lives. The trailers were like the US navy in Hawaii on December 6, 1941. We know what happened the next day. People usually only react after the incident.

On Friday, November 7, 2003, I drove to BIAP for goodies and supplies. We also stopped at the duty free—for the others, since neither Khalid nor I drank. Captain M was with us. On the way back, about halfway, we were directed off the main highway by Iraqi police with AK-47s. We ended up deep in the Red Zone. We drove parallel to the highway and ran in to a Bradley and a Humvee blocking the road. Since they were US troops, we asked what was going on. They had discovered an IED (improvised explosive device), which would have been detonated to disrupt traffic or destroy convoys. Captain M had on his helmet, pistol, and flak vest, like a good marine, but we told him to lose the helmet because he was conspicuous in the heavy traffic. The military gave us bad directions, and we were stuck going south in heavy traffic for about twenty-five minutes. We then found a place to turn around and kept trying to take the best roads we could find to the east. Eventually, we got back to our lines and the safety of the Green Zone, but we really got to see the city. I wish I'd had my camera. Khalid was driving, so I could have gotten some good shots; maybe next time. Khalid and Captain M were fine considering the tension, and I like to see that in a human. Khalid thought I was too friendly because I smiled at people, but I'd never been threatened. That night we watched *Ghost in the Darkness* with Kilmer and Douglas, an old movie but still good.

In the morning, we had new guards—all marines with Kevlar helmets and full battle gear. They were very imposing and would look good for the Marine Corps Ball on November 10 (the marine corps' birthday). I thought it was a total waste and a sham to cover up their incompetence. Good troops were wasted guarding palace "prissies" who were over-defended already. They should have been out anticipating guerilla and terrorist strikes. Sandbags for the compound, yes, but Delta Force, no!

The Red Cross announced it was leaving Baghdad and Basra, claiming it was too dangerous. They had been bombed with the four Iraq police stations a week earlier. One night, there was lots of rifle fire but no explosions. Maybe they were running low? I doubted it. When the moon waned, Ramadan would be over. I hoped they would find some other "hobbies" besides a class in creative explosives 107. (One of the rockets they shot at us was called a 107.) The Iraqi police got hit hard.

I respected the Iraqi police, who really earned their money.

Al Qaeda was blamed for a bomb in the Saudi Arabian capital, Riyadh, that killed two. Apparently, they disliked the Saudis for playing both sides of the fence (sending them money to support their projects and getting money from us by selling oil).

We set up our "illegal" satellite dish. In America, it would have been illegal, but in Iraq there were no cable or satellite companies. We bought a dish and decoder for $200, a TV for $380, a DVD for $150, and we were set. I watched *Windtalkers*, but it was in French (probably dubbed in Lebanon), which is kind of funny since the plot is all about language. Most of the channels had Arabic subtitles, but that didn't help me unless the actors were speaking English. I was a First World denizen in a Third World country and was treated like a second-class citizen. We watched *Predator* and made the Pop Secret microwave popcorn my daughter Cristen had sent me. Amal gave me a keychain with my name on one side and inshallah (if God wills it) in Arabic on the other.

Monday, November 10, was Jarhead Day (the Marine Corps' birthday). During the night, I was awakened by loud noises; it was not mortars, just good old thunder. It rained on the roof (loud in the trailers), but it was comforting, and the dry sand ate the moisture up quickly. I had always liked storms, and it was nice to experience one again.

We would soon get a change of command; the bird colonel was bringing around his replacement bird colonel. I didn't know what type of show we had to put on, but I was ready. We strung fiber to the fifth and sixth floor for the data and phones. Later, we would install switches and patch cords for the new PCs as the carpet and furniture was moved in. The wall painting was just about done. I tested and evaluated help-desk software (basically a database), and it was about as exciting as watching paint dry. I found that inshallah was an effective excuse for everything. Whenever we were pressed for a deadline, inshallah applied. When I saw someone establishing a pecking order (especially man over woman), and the emotion was evident in their voices, I'd interject "inshallah," and they'd both usually laugh. I know I was politically incorrect, but they knew instinctively that I meant them no harm, so I was tolerated and enjoyed as comic relief.

A worm sent an ICMP (pinging that caused unnecessary traffic on network), and even though there were only few users, it was very slow. We went from machine to machine and ran the antivirus program to stop the assault. I had planned to teach Basim how to drive with a stick shift, but he was pretty busy killing the worm. The sandbag idea had taken root, but unfortunately these people had never been in combat and did not use logic. The more beds you can segregate with sandbags, the less killing power the rocket or mortar round has. The trailers were made of cheap sheet metal and would only add to the shrapnel in an explosion. The misguided sandbag engineers did not do much good. They did not go around the trailers, and only if the mortar or rocket is considerate enough to stay outside the trailer area would the sandbags do any good. From the air, the trailer looked like a letter *H* with the people sleeping in the legs and arms of the *H*. If sandbags had been stacked window high, like the letter *C*, around each end of the legs, then a mortar or rocket hit would kill two at most. But due to where they placed the sandbags, up to twenty would have been hit if a rocket or mortar round landed in the middle.

*It took two months of pointing out the obvious to
the brass to get this simple task done.*

One night, I went to bed early, around 10:00 p.m., and wouldn't you know it, we got shelled. I knew it was close because of the vibration in the trailer. The parking lot bought it, and around twenty vehicles were toast. Fortunately, our Galloper had not been parked there. I didn't have my camera when they hauled away the wreckage. At least, the insurgents didn't forget us on Veteran's Day.

Khalid, most of the staff, and I went to the Green Zone restaurant for pizza, roast chicken, and kabobs. The party broke up at 7:30 p.m. When they joked in Arabic, I had to rely on emotions and gestures. At 9:19 p.m., we heard sixty-four mortar explosions. (You begin to count after a while, kind of like when my dad sneezes.) I don't know what got hit or where, but it was not near the GOIC. We found out later that they had bombed and killed eighteen Italians and eight Iraqis in Nasiriya. The sixty-four hits we counted were the attacks in southeast Baghdad in retribution for the killing at a suspected gathering. Khalid got himself a car, so I had the Galloper SUV to myself. There was a petrol place behind the palace.

Something in the climate made me short-tempered, because I started to flare more at people's stupidity. The refrigerator was unplugged again, and the coffee pot was in its spot. I told Khalid this was unforgivable a second time and I would not tolerate another attempt on my life. I really think I was angry because my pop was warm, not because the insulin was spoiled. Khalid turned into a sultan; he bought furniture—a couch and TV table along with a new impressive desk—and fresh flowers for the office. It's all to save face. I had to ride to unload my pent-up frustration. I usually was a much happier and laid-back person. I thought that maybe launching a Christian crusade to retake the Garden of Eden (at the junction of the Tigris and Euphrates Rivers) was in order. I also thought about just getting a gun card (civilian permission to carry weapons) and going to kill something.

On Monday, November 17, Franz, head of the GSCS (a middle east Manpower company) Iraqi workers and a subcontractor from South Africa, was sick, and our power was out. I took five Iraqis to visit Franz at his house and then went back to work on documenting how to bring the electric back up with the generators. They all enjoyed their trip, and as we left everyone shook Franz's hand. I started to, but then I quickly pulled away and said, "Don't touch me!" Everyone was shocked for a second, and then they all laughed, realizing I was teasing.

Two days later, Franz still had the Iraqi crud. He went back and forth to the hospital and was gone from work for ten days. Last night, we attacked the Iraqis pretty hard. I was curious to see what CNN.com would say. FYI, I counted 152,564 coalition forces. Here's how it broke down (I did not count planned or promised troops):

United States: 130,000
New Zealand: 61 (engineers)
South Korea: 675 noncombatants
Portugal: 120 police
Romania: 800 including 100 Military Police and 149
    landmine engineers
Philippines: 177
United Kingdom: 7,400
Norway: 156 (engineers and mine cleaners)
Thailand: 400
Denmark: 406
Netherlands: 1,106 (650 marines); 230 engineers, MPs, and
    commandos
Slovakia: 82 (engineers)
Ukraine: 1,640
Italy: 3,000
Czech Republic: 296 (civilians, MPs, and at the Basra field
    hospital)
Poland: 2,400
Hungary: 300
Albania: 71 (noncombatants)
Macedonia: 28:
Bulgaria: 485
Moldavia: 24-plus (landmine engineers)
Georgia: 69
Estonia: 55
Latvia: 106
Lithuania: 90
Azerbaijan: 150 (MPs)

Kazakhstan: 27
El Salvador*: 360
Dominican Republic*: 300
Honduras*: 360
Nicaragua*: 120
Spain*: 1,300

All the asterisked countries were attached to Spain in south central Iraq. Oman sent a battalion to Kuwait for protection, but I didn't count them. Thirty-four countries were involved at some level. The US numbers are all inclusive but contain civilians, police, and reserve units.

Khalid had a driver who wore a suit like a Mafia guy; he even had a 1960s razor cut, like a short, dry Fonzie cut, but I did not see a weapon.

On the morning of Friday, November 22, Iraqi terrorists launched a unique attack on the Sheraton Hotel. They strapped rockets and bombs to donkeys. The attack of the asses began. There was donkey meat everywhere, and it was another effective attack on the Green Zone. Like the fake generator they had used on the Al Rasheed a couple of weeks earlier, this caught the force protection off guard. Only two were wounded, and there were no deaths. Many of the rockets were diffused and didn't work. They left one donkey that looked like he'd had a rough night, with his own personal ass burned by rocket exhaust.

Covering Michael (part of force protection) in the Red Zone.

Instead of eating lunch, I went to downtown Baghdad with Michael (force protection), Jim (a contractor doing remodeling for the State Department), Dr. Ed, and Mohammed from the GSCS. We were looking for a custom leather shop; we wanted leather coats. We went the way the Iraqis go, and it was slow and long. They are not allowed on the 14th of July Bridge, so we meandered through Baghdad. We looked on the Internet to find a map of downtown. I took pictures as we went, and we talked about the exploding asses. We saw a donkey cart and said it was a terrorist attack vehicle. Michael had his leather coat measured while he was wearing his bulletproof jacket, and I kept the weapon and watched the door. We got back using the 14th of July Bridge and our CPA and DoD passes.

Michael covers me in the Red Zone while I get fitted for a new coat.

My trailer shuddered some nights from the rocket or mortar concussions. I actually enjoyed the danger; it was invigorating until it actually tore flesh. It was like driving a car to its limit; you want to go to the edge but not over. At the edge, you feel the most alive after a close encounter.

The following Sunday, all was quiet again. It seemed almost ludicrous. I injected myself with a sanitized needle and a fly landed on my exposed stomach. The contrast between the environment and the antiseptic process required for diabetes was ridiculous. Intellectual pursuit could not thrive there; most of the time, the people were engaged in basic survival. Shoes and socks took a backseat to food. Ramadan was a necessity, for the goal of the fast is to give food to the less fortunate. I liken this to the Catholic requirement in the late first millennium to eat fish on Fridays.

Most poor Catholics were fishermen, so the church boosted their economies by adding this religious law.

Eid is the opposite of Ramadan; everyone gets to pig out. The night before Eid is the night of destiny. It is supposed to be a prayer night, but it was interpreted by some as an attack night. The actual night depended on the lunar calendar, which was interpreted by the clerics. After Eid, I expected it to be less combative, but I hoped they wouldn't lose the creativity they'd used to devise the generator and donkey attacks. Maybe we would have a night of mortars on the dogs' backs. The Shiite Eid began the day after the Sunni's Eid. I think they deliberately are different so each sect can say its way is best.

Khalid went to Dubai to meet his parents for Eid. The airport had been closed since the Iraqi rocket hit the DHL plane, and Air Jordan was no longer running. Khalid wanted to make his reserved flight from Jordan to Dubai, so he hired a driver to take him.

The GSCS staff obtained permission to take out the SK staff before Eid. I was full and really didn't want to go, but they were so looking forward to the White Palace Restaurant (a five-star rating to them). It was deep in the Red Zone, on the southeast side, east of the Tigris River. They told me to hide my IDs and that it was dangerous. I drove the Galloper, and traffic was a zoo, with no traffic laws and everyone trying to dominate. Thank God for my expert training in Chicago's rush hour; a lesser driver would have snapped. My guys tried to scare me by saying how bad it was and that I would be shot. I told them, "You are the ones in trouble by hanging out with me. If an Iraqi aims at me, chances are he would miss and only hit people near me, because Iraqis were such bad shots." That logic shut them up.

We double parked where there was no room. We locked the car but left it in neutral for the parking guys. They would just pushed it back and forth to let people out. The restaurant was nice and clean, although I never got used to Kleenex boxes instead of napkins. I had lamb champ, which is like baked Alaska in a big puff, with a spicy and steamy center of rice, lamb, and chicken. The vegetables were nicely cut, cooked red beets with parsley, radishes, fresh cucumbers, and cabbage in olive oil. Silverware was strategically placed in serving dishes around the table, but they mostly used table spoons for everything we'd use a fork for. There were probably only five forks for fifteen people, but I had no trouble getting one.

The power went out in the quadrant, but because it was a nice restaurant, we were up and running in ten minutes on diesel power. After dinner, no one wanted to go with me, and I wasn't sure where the 14th of July Bridge was. So Basim rode with me until we were near the Green Zone; I dropped him off at a taxi stand when I could see the GOIC.

The Gurkhas were getting harassed back home by the Maoists, who had crossed into Nepal from China. These Communist rebels/criminals extorted money from the Gurkha families. It was approximately $10,000 each; interestingly, that was the exact amount Gurkhas would take home after their two-year stint in Iraq. I let the Gurkhas use my cell phone to call home to get morale support, and they sent money home, $2,000 or so at a time, to keep their families safe. "At the end of the tour," I told them, "get together in a group and kill the Maoists with the official blessing of Katmandu [the capital of Nepal]." Unfortunately their prince was afraid of the Gurkhas and wouldn't allow them to take their weapons back. Their families were in constant fear, and all the men were in foreign countries. Most news agencies were not concerned with a small country like Nepal. I ate lunch with and gave rides to the Gurkhas, and a lot of them knew me. Once, I was walking by the back entrance of the palace, and a troop of fifty Gurkhas were marching by. They stopped and waved to me saying, "Hello, sir," and other positive salutations. I'm sure the marines looking on thought I was a "somebody" to deserve that much attention.

At Thanksgiving, President Bush visited with the troops at the BIAP from about 7:00 to 8:00 p.m.; they had dinner. Lots of choppers were up during 5:30 to 8:00 p.m. period he was there. We drew lots at the GOIC to see who would go to meet W, but I didn't get to see him. Still, I was impressed that he'd made the effort. I actually voted for him because he had the guts to go to Iraq and serve turkey to the troops. He was definitely a favored Iraqi target. Baker, the administrator in charge, said he was going to read the president's Thanksgiving message and asked if there were anyone of higher rank in the audience who might do so. The president appeared from the crowd and received a big ovation. The GOIC guy who won the draw took his bodyguards and a trunk of RPGs(Rocket Propelled Grenades similar to the American Bazooka), side arms, and an AK-47. They did not let him meet the president.

I had taken Jon (a Raytheon employee) to the airport earlier; he flew his girlfriend from New Orleans to Amman, Jordan, for a five-day tryst. Air Jordan cancelled his flight, and he was distraught because he'd spent $2,500 on her ticket and $815 for his own. I put him in touch with Franz, who knew a Jordanian driver who could take Jon to Amman. He was scared about driving six hours across Iraq—it was two hours from the border to Amman—but it was mostly desert, and I gave him a book to read. Besides, when salmon are swimming upstream, they don't think about rocks. He would have a great story to tell his girl, and she could comfort him.

My roommate left, and the trailer was mine. We had enough issues without incompetents like him. Every time a car door closed at night, he ran to the palace basement to hide. If he heard a report about an impending attack, he took cover. He was a black Muslim from the Bronx and an ex-air force enlisted man with SATCOM experience. Unfortunately, his experience wasn't with the kind of dish we used in Iraq. Robert tried to convert me to Islam, and I listened as he told me Muslims are one with God.

I told him, "Then I am a Muslim, but I am not Islamic. I'm from the 'God is a spare tire' school, and organized religion is for the aggrandizement of organized religion, not God."

He couldn't grasp my concepts and I didn't hold a lot of stock in his. He told me about Ramadan and Eid and how you were supposed to fast—no liquids, smoking, sex or food during daylight hours—with a small repast allowed after prayer in the pre- and post-daylight hours. The extra food was to go to the poor. I watched him volunteer for night shift and sleep all day during the Ramadan and had to say, "Practice what you preach."

When Steve came to replace Robert, he told Robert to leave and that he didn't need any "up to speed time" from him. In the meantime, Robert had developed an e-mail empire, similar to Hitler's nonexistent armies in March 1945 that he was "running" in six countries. After Steve told him to leave, Robert became even more estranged and withdrawn.

A new man came in, Dave; Robert proceeded to buddy up with him on the phone. I lent our vehicle to Robert one morning so he could pick up Dave at BIAP. As they were coming back, I talked to them on the phone and said I would meet them at the front gate to save a security check, and then I would take them back to the palace. I had told Steve the previous night that Robert should leave the country, that he was very troubled and could have some issues. I was surprised he hadn't left already, as fearful as he had been during his short stay. Dave and Robert went through gate security and drove halfway around the building, where I was walking to meet them at the gate. They stopped and demanded the vehicle for the rest of the day, saying they were managers and had important company business to do. I told them it was the GOIC's vehicle, to be used to carry supplies and parts, and I had to pick some project parts at the airport. They said they were taking the vehicle.

I told Dave, "Stay out of it. You are new and don't understand the situation at all."

"I'm taking it," Robert said.

"No way," I said. "It's my vehicle, and you have worn out your welcome."

But Robert charged off in the vehicle, in open defiance of my wishes and protestations. I was visibly upset. I walked to the nearest Gurkha and asked him to call the front gate and stop the renegade managers from executing their plans. The trusty Gurkhas easily foiled their plot and brought them back with the vehicle; Robert and Dave were forced out at gunpoint. In their haste to comply with the Gurkhas' wishes, they locked their personal supplies and my keys in the Galloper. Robert, in his infinite wisdom, wanted to break the window to retrieve Dave's luggage.

I was still livid and said, "No. Dave can run around naked for all I cared because parts here are very difficult to acquire, but idiots are bountiful."

I went inside to get a hanger to open the car door. I returned and bent it properly so it would fit through the door insulation. I gave the hanger to Robert and went to talk briefly to Khalid. I told the Gurkhas to shoot them if they tried to start the car. Both Robert and Dave were visibly shaken, as I said it quite adamantly. I returned within two minutes; the door was open, and both of them were standing far away from the Galloper, with the Gurkhas looking on. Khalid told me to leave them and let them walk back, but I figured the new guy had all his bags and was just caught up in Robert's issues. I asked them where they wanted to go, and they directed me to a location where they had an appointment, so I dropped them off. I'd no sooner returned when I received a call from Sneak and Snitch (i.e., Dave and Robert). They didn't have an appointment after all; the customer wasn't even there.

I was not happy with these two idiots, but because Dave was new and had his entire overseas luggage, I returned and picked them up. This time I dropped them off at the palace. Dave returned, sans Robert, to the GOIC in the evening, saying he was okay and Robert was off key. The next day Dave called the office and told Washington DC that we had booze in our office. (That was funny because neither Khalid nor I drank). In Vietnam, we fragged (threw a fragmentation grenade) people like that in their sleep, especially when they put their comrades at risk. We knew then that it wasn't just that Robert was estranged. We thoroughly ostracized Dave, and he had no visiting privileges. I saw him after Robert was forced to exit the country and viewed him as one would a dog turd in his path—it was of no consequence, I just had to be careful not to step in it (get involved). The home office called, and in the final analysis we were okay, and they were admonished.

The next day I went to the GOIC and found that Khalid was hiring a new secretary. He had been complaining about Shams (whose work was shoddy), and she was in love with him and said so to everyone. I paid $90/month toward her salary in a month, but she really worked for Khalid and wasn't interested in me or my needs. She ironed his shirts and ran whatever errand he gave her, but also dusted the keyboard while the computer was running (consequently, putting many unreadable words on the screen). Khalid decided to let Shams go (from a business standpoint), but also because he could hire an attractive secretary, who spoke English better, at $440/month. Shams had been paid $200/month and thus lost the income for her family. Her sister was an Iraqi policewoman, but that paid only $60/month. Their rent was $100/month for their mom and the three girls, who were between eighteen and twenty years old. They weren't charged for utilities, but they didn't always work. Everyone burned his garbage, and gas was cheap (about eleven cents a gallon), so people who could afford a generator bought one. But Shams's family could not. She was very thin and wore the scarf over her head, like many Islamic women, but she was intelligent. Like all women of twenty, she was focused on her future mate and how to obtain him.

Secretary and policewoman.

There was a real balancing act between Islam and TV, and the women tried to stick to the rules they had been taught. (They were probably not much different than Catholic school girls.) But they still felt the hormones and saw the beautiful people in the movies or on MTV. Wanting love and the opportunity to find your place and your special someone is a universal desire. I believed the women were the real future of the country. The men kept them in line and continued the wars with Iran, Kuwait, and the United States, but without the women as enablers, the wars wouldn't happen. They support their men, right or wrong, in whatever capacity they can. *If we could educate them to fulfill useful middle-class roles*, I thought, *they would have the capacity for change and could lead their country out of its then-current status*. The men, I believed, would bring it back to the status quo and just change the players in power.

I felt bad for Shams, so I took her and Amal to the palace with Cato (a mercenary marine like Michael) to see the "deSaddamizing" of the palace. They had never been there as Iraqis when Saddam was in power, and like all women, they were curious to see the interior. I told them about the decapitation that was happening (i.e., the removal of five huge, bronze Saddam heads) and that they could get their pictures taken next to history. They had to be searched, signed in, and authenticated before they could traverse the palace grounds. We took pictures near the fountain, next to a downed bronze head, and in the palace by the ornate furniture. We looked at the palace inside and out.

Shams(Secretary), Amal(Teacher), Cato(Mercenary),
and me next to a decapitated Saddam.

The parts of those bronze busts sold very quickly on the Internet. I don't know who profited, but the new Iraqi government wanted them gone and didn't care how.

All five Saddams were removed from palace for political reasons.

Khalid asked me to move out of the office, and it really upset me, especially since Shams had just been let go. He told me he was "a dick" for doing it but thought it would be good for me to set up a test lab and work with Basim and Rah. He would take care of the TV, DVD, satellite, and refrigerator. I didn't understand but decided that I would do it for the project. To attract my interest, he showed me three different offices and offered me part of Amal's training area, which I turned down. I eventually decided on the big office in the center of the building. We were back in the office, and he was barking orders, and it hit me: Khalid didn't care if I were close to Basim and Rah; he wanted me out so he could be alone with his secretary. I was really mad, not because he wanted me out but because he had played me instead of just telling me what he wanted to do. I said, "You told me you were a dick, and you are. I'm leaving because I won't be good company tonight." I went to the gym to hit the bike and work off the issues.

The next morning, I moved my stuff and the equipment for the audio project. I had to get rid of stuff and get more stuff. (I had eight desks and one table in my office.) I saw Shams moping around, trying to get any kind of a job with the governing council. She could type and had basic computer skills, thanks to Amal. Abu Jacob asked me to hire her. At first I said no, but then I thought, *Why not?*

Twenty-five mikes with recording ability but controlled by the secretary general

I decided the next day to hire Shams, and if she got a government job that was fine. I told her I could pay $150 but she would have to really clean. I then looked into getting English lessons for her, and I thought I could get her a special tutor if I could arrange transportation. It would have to have a minimum impact on us, as I couldn't assign GOIC drivers to shuttle her around. Shams was pleased to have the opportunity and said she would no longer pursue the government position. "Keep looking for a better position," I told her, "because I may not always be here, and I want you to be Iraq's president in twenty years."

We began to tackle the cleaning of my new office, and she did a commendable job. We involved other workers in the building, and I gave everyone Coca-Cola Light and malted milk balls. (I guess I was like the ugly American with the Hershey bars, just a different generation.) They vacuumed the overhead, got sugar out of the carpet, and moved all kinds of furniture and equipment around. I'd never seen Shams work so hard. When we were installing the refrigerator and microwave, I couldn't get the DC plug to fit in to the socket. She cut the end of the plug off, stripped the wires, took a pen and pushed it into the ground socket, and placed the wires inside. When she released the pen, it locked in place and worked fine. I'm sure her skills developed from practice in a poor electrical environment, but I was still amazed.

At the end of the day, she was waiting to get a ride from one of the guys upstairs and indicated that she knew how to play chess. Okay, I figured. She played a very good game and gave me a good run. No one knew how intelligent she was. I thought the language lessons would give her additional skills to get what she wanted and change the quality of her and her family's lives.

My chai(tea) maker with the hat I had made in the United States.

The chai man (tea maker), Abu Jacob, was older, so I got him Centrum Silver vitamins and told him to take one every other day. I hoped that would supplement him well; I told him it was old man's rejuvenation medicine. I had a color printer, and I printed pictures I'd taken of the people. They loved the attention, and the pictures I took of Amal and Shams in the palace generated a lot of interest. I told them Shams was a wife of Saddam and Amal was a queen. I took pictures of them drinking chai and sitting on various thrones.

Steve, Jim, Rich, a different Dave, and I planned a trip to Basra, which was near the seaport to the south held by the British. The Tigris and Euphrates come together just to the northwest of there, and that's the supposed site of the original Garden of Eden.

But the trip was cancelled because Saddam had been caught, and life was dangerous for a few days. Many people were firing guns in the air; one young Iraqi walked out of the Al Rasheed after work and was brought down by a wayward celebratory round piercing his cranium. I questioned people there, and they were apprehensive but relieved Saddam had been captured. Many Iraqis had felt Saddam was done in April 2003 when he ran. Someone car bombed the Hotel Baghdad with gasoline, so he was clearly desperate for attention. There were three car bombs at the edge of the Green Zone, but two failed. It was not for want of trying, but I thought their technical staff was weak. Three GOIC councilmen interviewed Saddam on Iraqi TV and asked him if he were sorry about killing the Chestman (a cleric). Saddam said the cleric was not a chest but a foot, which is a big insult in the Middle East. When they asked him if he were sorry for attacking Kuwait, he said "No, Kuwait should be part of Iraq." He said he had no regrets. I think his attitude was, "What are you going to do now that you don't have me to kick around?" He was right, and after he was incarcerated, a true power vacuum developed. Religious figures and government officials all tried to get the power. Shiites, Kurds, Sunni, and maybe even ex-Ba'ath party members vied for the lead roles.

The parade grounds had many commemorations. I climbed up through the trapdoor at the base of the north sword and climbed half way up and could see the GOIC. If I had been smaller, I could have gotten to the top.

I climbed up the swords using the underground access.

Shams learned all of our names and could spell them on the blackboard. We had a Christmas party at the Al Rasheed Sports Bar. I was allowed to take up to four Iraqi staff members, but I had to sign them in. I took Shams and the interpreter, Redhab (a Kurdish woman), Steve had hired. Shams, as a Muslim, usually didn't wear makeup and wore the traditional hijab worn by Muslim women. But she did like American glamour and movie magazines, so she had Redhab put makeup on her. We went to the party, and there were snacks and drinks. The girls ordered pop, as I did, while the rest all had beer or mixed drinks. I don't think Shams and Redhab liked the food, but we had the white-elephant-type of gift giving in which everyone puts a wrapped ten-dollar gift (gag or not) under the tree. We all drew numbers—there were thirty-two of us—and whoever got 1 went first. He or she could pick any present but couldn't touch it before selecting it. Once a gift was selected, the person opened it and sat to the side. Number 2 then could take number 1's present or select a new one to open. If your gift was stolen, you could take a number and steal another gift (not your old one) or open a new one. After a few gifts had been opened, people would trade (e.g., a guy with lip gloss might trade with a girl holding a cigar), and a gift could be stolen only three times. If you were the third person to take the same present, you returned to your seat with your prize. This continued until all the presents had been opened, and then you kept what you have. I told the girls it was an Ali Baba Christmas, because in Iraq they called thieves Ali Baba. The girls got okay gifts but had them stolen; Redhab traded for crayons and paper and got to keep them, while Shams stole someone's magic brass lamp (used when making strong coffee). Steve got girl's lip gloss, so when a girl came up to get a new gift, he put a twenty-dollar bill on it to get her to Ali Baba his so he could pick something else. Everyone was trying to peddle his or her trash and capture a radio or whatever was deemed a good gift. Sal, my counterpart in the building next door to GOIC, and I gave Redhab and Shams our numbers, so we sat out. Modifying a custom was fun for both sides, even those who were just watching.

We expected trouble, so we wanted the girls out before sunset. Shams was fine with that and more concerned about taking off the makeup so her mom wouldn't see it when she got home. (She reminded me of my Cristen in junior high.) Every one of the Iraqis had to leave, so I got Shams to her ride, but Redhab wanted to watch *It's a Wonderful Life* on the sports bar screen. I came back and watched the end of the movie with her, and then it was dark. The missiles began to fall, and I got word there were four insurgent teams working around the Green Zone to harass our Christmas celebration. We went into the GOIC—Steve, Dave #2, Redhab, and me. I told her not to worry, because the building was safe and she didn't need to be in a taxi right then. One Russian-made, 80 mm rocket hit the roof of the third floor, over my office, but did not explode. I have the exhaust port from the rear of it, which looks like an old distributor cap. Things calmed down around 8:30 p.m. so Michael ran Redhab to the taxi stand so she could get home. The girls were off till Saturday, December 27. I went back to the trailer, and around 11:00 p.m., the attacks really started. They used a Spectre, a night-attack plane with mini-guns and other goodies. Religion was a factor there, so our season was going to be ruined by them, no matter what.

We had been getting shelled a lot, and my trailer got to rocking Christmas night with three straight that lasted well into the morning of December 26. Two grunts (army infantrymen) bought it from mortar fire. There was a wooded area to the south of here that they used as a launch site. The army didn't want to go out in the Red Zone to ambush the bad guys for fear of too much exposure. I said, "Just napalm the woods, and they won't be able to use it for covert activities anymore." Another possibility was to have the navy seals bury some C-4 with ball bearings and a remote detonator in those woods. When they launched, we set off the explosives.

On Sunday, December 28, sadly I had to let Redhab go. She was using Michael's and Cato's names to motivate people and had altercations with Iraqi police and government security people. As much as I liked her, she had to go. Steve and Dave #2 had hired her to teach them Arabic, and I was to house her at the GOIC during the day. She was to learn how to use the computer and teach Shams English. Everyone thought I had hired a "sexcretary," especially after I took them to the Christmas shindig. I explained to Amal and Abu Jacob that Steve and Dave had hired her. I explained that in America, a boss who uses secretary for sex is accused of sexual harassment and is sent to court. I gave Redhab a month's pay and a note explaining her shortcomings and issues she'd created. I wished her well and good fortune. I let Shams read the note, because I had written that even though she and Redhab were supposed to teach each other, they would just talk and goof off. Shams profited by Redhab's short employment and saw that sexuality isn't as important as diligent effort. Her work ethic had risen dramatically since she was hired by Khalid. I hoped she would survive her environment and use her natural intelligence to help her people. She knew poor, and now she knew work and had some taste of self-sufficiency. I envisioned that she would get to pride of a job well done and a good feeling of accomplishment, as she learned English and saw success from her labors.

MRE (meals ready to eat) are what today's soldiers get instead of K-rations or C-rations. Inside is a long plastic bag with a silver-like plate, the size of a hand mirror; when it is slightly covered with water, it causes a reaction that heats the water up much like a car battery works with the plates to create electricity. I had several cases of MREs in my office, and I gave them to those who were hungry or used them to bribe people. I was very careful to keep the pork ones or give them to Christian Iraqis. I showed an MRE to one of the Iraqis, who was skeptical of its ability to get hot. When it began to steam, he was fascinated, like a little kid who had found something really cool. Pretty soon, I had a minor riot, with all the people wanting to see the magic heater. What started as a practical demonstration turned into a full Disney production. Everyone was talking at a hundred miles an hour, wanting to see it work, and the ones who had seen it wanted to show the ones who hadn't. We went through a dozen MRE heaters before I was done. I had to explain that they could not eat, drink, or make tea with it because it was for heat only and quite poisonous. I made sure the instructions were repeated in Arabic so there would be no mistakes.

I took Shams to the airport, where she had her first Burger King sandwich (chicken royale with cheese). Considering that she had grown up there, and lived only ten miles from the airport, she was impressed by BIAP. She really hadn't seen much of her own world. I bought her a pair of Nike shoes to replace her homemade clogs. She put them on when we got back from BIAP, and while she was showing them off, another crazy riot ensued. Arab voices were going a hundred miles an hour; I heard the word "shoes" every so often. The next day she didn't wear them, and when I questioned her, she said she got them dirty in the mud at her home. I was worried she'd gotten mugged for the shoes, but I think she was upset because they were dirty.

On New Year's Eve, people got ready for a two-day holiday. (They were always off on Friday.) I'd been in Iraq for well over a quarter of a year, and I felt the people were making progress. However, the governing council, like most politicians, was composed of more of the same. Council members seemed more interested in perpetuating their own existence than on accomplishing their jobs—to write a new constitution. Change is a slow process.

There was a great deal of celebratory fire that night, and I watched from the roof with Dave #2, Steve, Michael, Cato, and Ann (Cato's friend from the ambassador's office) It amazed me how people so dirt poor could have so much expensive ammo after all that time. It had been more than eight months since Saddam left Baghdad, and yet we still had a Red Zone and armed resistance. *They are going to have to treat the populace like the Germans after WWII*, I thought, *and disarm and reeducate.*

The Gurkhas dragged me off the next afternoon around 2:30 p.m., saying it was no big deal and I had to go with them. We ended up behind the generators toward the back gate, and they were cooking in the open with a picnic table and plenty of flies. They were drinking Scotch (mixed with strawberry Fanta for the new guys and straight for the old vets) and Carlsberg beer. They made a curry-like gravy and cooked very bone-chip-laden beef or goat meat (both, I think) and put that over white rice. They made a very spicy vegetable dish, and I mixed it all together. I had to eat with care because of all the bone chips, but it was quite tasty, spicy hot and yet chilled. Cato didn't eat much of it but Michael and I both did. Michael and I went back to the office and watched *Bend It like Beckham*, which is a good PG-13 movie about soccer and cross-cultural conflicts. The Iraqis liked it because they had similar cultural values.

After the celebratory fire on New Year's Day, my trailer roof was penetrated by an AK-47 round. My roof would have leaked if I didn't get it fixed, but other than that, there was no damage. It wasn't as bad as Vietnam, where my hooch was blown up with me in it. But you have to believe in a higher power of some sort when you are continually spared.

I wrote up a job description for Shams and tried (with Steve) to get SK to hire her. That way, if I were gone, she would still be okay. I used our GSCS people for comparison and put her on the bottom rung for money but with raises quarterly, providing she was successful in her English education and computer classes. Amal said she would teach Shams Advanced Word and Basic Excel.

It was nice to have a quiet night. I heard the security guys talking, and it was like a war was going to breakout. I talked to others, and they said it would calm down. Iraq was like politics: everyone had an opinion.

The Galloper started leaking oil and coolant. I told Dr. Ed, and he finally took it to be repaired, so for two days I rode the bus. Then he got me a Suzuki, but I had to walk half a mile into the Red Zone to get it. He was as unarmed as was I, and he said I could stay back. But I knew that would be bad from a saving-face point of view, so I went with him.

The Suzuki had a leak in the radiator, but it did run. I got fuel at the depot, even though the car had local plates. I think they thought I was a spy or counterintelligence guy. On the way back from the airport, the car's engine began to knock loudly. As we approached, the Green Zone's early checkpoint, it died. I coasted until I was a half mile from the Green Zone and pulled over so I would not block the exit. Unfortunately, that was also the turnaround site for all the Iraqis who weren't allowed to go into the Green Zone. Steve had my .45 pistol while I was driving, so I told him to stay in the car with Shams while I stood outside with half a brick to throw (if necessary) but mostly to look in control and casual until Cato could pick us up. The sheer volume of Red Zone traffic was amazing. Steve stayed in the backseat with the pistol drawn but hidden from view, and Shams sat in the front seat looking straight ahead. Cato arrived within fifteen minutes, and we pushed the Suzuki to the side of the road, loaded ourselves and our stuff into his vehicle, and headed off for the GOIC. I got a new, white Galloper after that incident.

My staff gave me a plate with this image.

Saddam's son Uday had a palace-like place, where he interrogated and punished people as he saw fit. These seven lions were part of his interrogation process.

Uday's frisky lions.

The remains of a child who had been consumed by lions.

*Prisoners were fed like dogs and lived in cages
so small, they were unable to stand.*

Uday liked to have a woman submit, but if she resisted, her husband was sent to the human pound and her child might be thrown in with the lions while she watched. We saw the pelvis of a four-year-old boy to whom that had happened. I arrived in Iraq right after Qusay and Uday were killed with the rocket. I saw the pictures during and after with their riddled bodies and mangled legs. Not pretty but biblical in the sense of an eye for an eye. Iraq is a very harsh country.

After Uday's demise, his eighty-car luxury fleet was stolen and restolen by local militia and bandits. They would drive the roads and attack others; then in turn they would be shot in the car, and the "new" owners would drive and kill until the car couldn't drive or was sold in Syria. Bush made a mistake by not retaining the Iraqi Army on their sixty-dollar-per-month salaries, and soon most of the quickly retired Republican Guard were terrorists or bandits for hire. Officially every household was allowed an AK-47. If RPGs and AK-47s had been confiscated and the Republican Guard and police had been issued shotguns, people's ammo would have been useless and the bad guys easily identified. This would have greatly curtailed the death of and harm to Iraqi citizens

George, the world's top SATCOM combat troubleshooter.

George was summoned by the coalition to troubleshoot the fiber between the IT in the palace and our dish and shed. He got paid by the hour in hundreds and was always guaranteed a week's work. He would fly anywhere in the world at a moment's notice to fix a calamity and had homes in six countries. He had an understanding Korean wife and was the best tech I ever met. He did the unsolvable in four days and drank for three more. He slept very little but if you needed your system to work, he was the guy to get. He was very rich by the time I met him, and I found him very down to earth and funny.

Al Hillah

It was time for an archaeological trip. I wanted to see another location, and our nearest dish was in al Hillah, near Babylon. We drove in a convoy south through Baghdad.

Looking north to Baghdad.

On route we found some Iraqi tanks that had been destroyed in the April 2003 push to the capital.

Tanks destroyed on the route south of Baghdad.

Our rear guard behind us.

Expeditions are a way to see the people and the mood of a country. Many countries have an agenda when it comes to Iraq, usually not to help Iraqis but to help themselves. When you're an oil producer, you question a rich man's or a pretty girl's advances. In Iraq, there are a variety of tribes, each of which wants respect and power. Sunnis will not vote for a Kurd, no matter how qualified he is for the office. Arguments on each side have become mantras over the years and are repeated to the opposing side like a Hail Mary in church.

We arrived in al Hillah two and a half hours after leaving the palace area. We went to the hotel and the roof to check the dish.

Rich, Tim, and I check the view.

Everything was in order, and Tim was to stay there and run the dish for a while till SK could get a replacement. Steve and I went on with the troops to Babylon2 the Saddam renovated ruins.

The troops weren't allowed inside Babylon2.

Saddam had Babylon's front gate painted blue for
Pope John Paul, but he'd cancelled the trip.

Saddam had wanted to impress the world by having the pope visit Babylon, so he reconstructed it, but to me it seemed like an amusement park without the rides. The pope cancelled his visit, so maybe Saddam just didn't finish it; there was bad blood between them over the cancellation. The front gate was bright blue and decorated with yellow and white salukis (Arabian greyhounds) and horses.

The rebuilt walls; you can see the old ones at the bottom.

This part of the reconstructed Babylon2 seemed better done.

This was my favorite part and seemed a good recreation of the era.

We rode back with the troop convoy and returned to the palace after dark. I enjoyed the day in spite of the restoration done by Saddam's "engineers."

When we got back, I found out that Shams's mom was in the hospital with angina. In the United States, it is the least fatal of the heart ailments, but in Iraq, the hospital survival rate is considerably lower. It cost $2,000 if you want to be admitted right away, or you can wait a year or two to see if the "free one" (socialized medicine) is available. Steve and I had to go to the airport again. We went with the new vehicle and got a flat tire. It took almost a half hour to fix because we had to read the manual to find all the stuff (three different places). I got the trashed tire fixed the next day.

Mosul

A different Steve, another SK employee, got bored in Basra, so he recommended that we install a dish in Mosul in northern Iraq. He'd made friends with a colonel up there and stayed in a really nice hotel. I had to review and evaluate the network.

Northern Mosul was the site of the other oil center and was very important to the coalition. They had the pipeline, and everyone wanted a piece. The northern commander was very adamant that the dish be placed in Erbil, a beautiful town in a non-arid climate that hosted the best hotel in Iraq. He wanted his headquarters there.

I returned to Mosul to examine the work areas for computers and wireless installation. They had concrete walls, and it was difficult to drill for wire, so they really wanted wireless. I recommended against it because the concrete was so thick the signals couldn't pass through it. Since a remote wireless access point (WAP) also required wires, I gave them a new wiring plan that just required two large holes and then the spread to various desk areas for connectivity. Their network worked okay, and I thought the dish should be close to the users. I caught a flight back, stopping in Sulaymaniyah (Kurd territory) and Samarra before returning to Baghdad.

Khalid was causing problems—selling satellite time illegally— so I went to Basra while the bosses dealt with him. I would not "testify" against him, because I had never seen him do it, but he was doing something that had nothing to do with SK business.

I had just gotten the Iraqi governing council to agree on a contract with the CPA. The head of the Ministry of Information and I got along very well. I put Shams on a project to draw the fourth floor in Visio (a graphics application) to give her respect among her own people. The fourth-floor governing council guys knew I was leaving soon, and they wanted my water cooler. I told them they could have it on one condition: that they all voted for Shams twenty years from then (2024) when she campaigned to be prime minister of Iraq. They laughed, and I said, "No way then." Then they all agreed. Even if they never voted for her, I knew they would hold her in esteem, which is hard for an Iraqi woman to obtain. Before I left, the head of the ministry hired Shams to work on the fourth floor. She cried when I told her about the position and that I was leaving. I asked her to keep up her English for the family and gave Abu Jacob money to give her each month. I didn't want her to squander her education money.

I was reassigned to Basra with Steve #2. After a time, he went to Mosul to help with the dish and then returned to the home office in the United States. Right after I left, Jon sent me the picture of the palace IT on fire, as viewed from our SATCOM shed. The wiring was always everywhere up there, with extensions in extensions and all over the floors. This time, the cause was not Iraqi troublemakers but good old-fashioned military incompetence.

*The palace on fire—the view from the shed the
week after I left for Basra in early 2004.*

Basra

The trip to Basra was about five to six hours in a car, barring any grief. Flying took a minimum of three days. You had to get a secure convoy to BIAP, a C130 to a British fort that was west of Basra, and then a convoy to Basra. I had to move all my stuff, and Franz, the South African guy I'd saved from dehydration, had to fly to Abu Dhabi, then to Kuwait, up to the British fort, and finally get a convoy to Basra Palace. We decided to take our gear and drive down in an Iraqi taxi (Chevy Suburban) in a half day. The trip was rough because the Spanish had quit the coalition because of a train bomb threat. We had to go through much more Iraqi-controlled territory.

These T-52s were left to rot in the desert when our planes were bombing. They had no radios and wood planks for seats.

Iraqi troops and police created a blockade by placing rocks half the size of a soccer ball in a pattern on the road. This forced drivers to go to a particular place where they could check IDs and ask for food or money. Each time a coalition force withdrew from an area, the local tribes quickly reestablished controls and income. Each tribe had its own flag. My favorite was the Wassup tribe in central eastern Iraq. It reminded me of the television show *Good Times*, in which JJ said "dy-no-mite" all the time.

Eastern central Iraq, home to the Wassup tribe.

My taxi driver during the trip from Baghdad to Basra.

We saw the locals, but no authorities anywhere. In some areas, very few people spoke English, but Franz could speak the local lingo. People washed their rugs and hung them out to dry in the front of their homes to show off. The local flag and those rugs were the only colors in view. The regular laundry was usually in the back and not in plain sight. The local leader always had a house with an impressive front to let everyone know and a tent inside in the Bedouin tradition. That was the place where he passed judgment. Old traditions die hard.

Franz and the GSCS boys, safe at their house in Basra outside the fort.

We arrived at the GSCS house in the Basra Red Zone after an uneventful five-hour road trip. I met some of the old Baghdad guys and new ones as well. After Franz's stuff had been unloaded, we proceeded to the palace/fort.

This was the British-controlled zone; security was tighter, and there were more protocols. They let us in, but we were scanned and dogged (checked by dogs to see if we had bombs). My luggage was checked as well. They were amazed I had driven from Baghdad and took us to the security office to get our fort IDs. Franz only got a GCSC ID, which was a small step up from an Iraqi national ID. He was not allowed in the fort and could not stay overnight. He could not even use the mess hall, but later I got him privileges. They gave me a great ID, because I had to run the SATCOM, phones servers, and network WAPs. I did not do the American satellite or communications, which were run by their security people. Unfortunately, they were considerably less skilled than I was.

I caught up with Steve #2, the then-current SATCOM guy at my company. He was a fun-loving guy. He couldn't get a decent clearance, because he'd lived with this girl in Cuba. He could assemble three-meter satellite antenna pretty well and loved to travel. He was friends with Paola, a nice Italian diplomat's daughter from Rome, who was stationed in Basra. She was fun and was always skiing somewhere, with her strawberry blonde hair blowing behind her. Then she'd return to her job helping the locals. I don't know if she was married or engaged, but she liked Steve #2, especially when she had wine. She was lost but interesting and full of spirit.

Steve #2 remained in charge for a while but he would be gone before the CPA turned over control to the State Department in June. There were only eight Americans in the whole fort, where many nationalities were represented: Danish police and dairy-food importers, Italians, Iraqi dignitaries, Fijian guards, New Zealand security, Australian regulars, the full British complement, Irish, French Foreign Legion, and police advisors from many places. The British had the connections for liquor, but the Americans forbade it. Apparently, throughout history, the British had provided rum rations for their sailors and troops. They had a cheesy bar set up in a one-room office with one bath and two tiny tables, but everyone drank just outside. There was a nicer bar by the river but that was a long haul away. I went a few times but preferred to stay closer.

A half-hour walk around the fort took me to the British commissary, a source for different types of snacks. I liked the British and their accents. Their food didn't impress me, but British nail clippers were considerably more efficient than ours, and I was glad I explored their store.

The British commissary in the south side of fort; we could shop in this tent.

As I did in all new locations, the first thing I did was the "as is" drawing. I had to know about everything on site, not only for reference but to plan for improvements and troubleshooting. I had my graphics programs with me (Visio, Harvard Graphics, etc.) and found an e-size plotter like the one in the map room in Baghdad. It took me a week to trace my connectivity, both wired and WAPs (which are similar to Wi-Fi). I had to make tape and numbers, so line 13 would have a 13 at the router and the destination port. That meant tracing every wire throughout the compound. This assisted us immensely later when we were troubleshooting after bad weather or hostile fire. I printed my results and codes after two weeks and all the brass were gaga over the printed plots. I kept it in my office for quick reference. People at the site were amazed, and after a while our network worked better than the British one. Other nations wanted to be on our network.

The Basra help desk: the Iraqis, Keith from
Canada, and Franz from South Africa.

Three of the Iraqi staff eventually made it to other countries, thanks to my training and mentoring. Two were married and stayed with family, and one disappeared. They began learning basic PC wiring and troubleshooting, and later I showed them basic servers and LAN management.

There was some wireless; Keith, my Canadian CISCO phone expert, had set it up. The WAPS had two "channels," one for phones and the other for data. Keith handled the phone extremely well. We did updates and compressions and soon had a well-oiled communications system. I could get improved parts from my company, but it usually took a month or so to get a "rush" delivery. We had a help desk of six to seven Iraqis, several of whom were very intelligent. Dolfakar had a master's in fiber technology. Hamid and Basil were quick witted and amenable to learning. More important, all three had excellent English skills. Unfortunately, there were no computer-tech books in Arabic at that time. I got computer books for dummies and idiots, which explained concepts well. My tech manuals on TCP/IP(Transmission Control Protocol/Internet Protocol the basis for the internet and it's rules) were a little harder for them. Franz was a manager for GSCS and also mentored the boys. He had a computer outside the fort but not on our network.

The Iraqis were recruited by the GSCS system based in the United Arab Emirates (UAE), and all but one was from Basra. Dolfakar had been found cleaning toilets at the fort for the British at $60 per month (anything to bring money into the family). They became instant heroes with their families when they started earning $350 per month with their new jobs. When I updated equipment, I kept the old ones for them to practice on and created a teaching network so they could learn all aspects. My top three guys were placed in Great Britain, San Francisco, and Dubai within three years of my tutelage and recommendations and introduction letters. Basim, who was from Baghdad, took a temp job in Germany with Siemens, a big phone company. He also really liked German girls.

Hard workers from Pakistan, most of them were our chefs.

Baghdad Revisited

I was just starting to enjoy the vegetable curry made by our Pakistani cooks when I received a call from the home office stateside. The GOIC was no longer affiliated with DoD, and the Iraqis were going to negotiate the contract. The military echelon was having difficulty closing the deal and were frustrated after Khalid was ousted to Jordan. Both sides knew and trusted me, so I returned to the GOIC. They gave me my own trailer. I was an equivalent GS-13, and I got a GS-15 accommodation for almost a month. It was very nice; instead of sharing one bath with four others, I had my own bath and shower and a living room besides my bed and desk. (It was posh but short-lived.) I worked with the Iraqi head of IT, who was young for such a top position (and had haunting green eyes). He'd had to live in Turkey during Saddam's tirades.

Shams was very happy to see me. She had visibly changed; her clothing was more modern, and her scarf more colorful. She wore makeup and carried a cell phone. She still worked for the interim government and now traveled with a mass of young friends. She was still taking English lessons. My trusty chai maker Abu Jacob was still there, and he paid extra special attention to me and my chai, which raised eyebrows among the newer government delegates. He had his wife make me this huge hand-carved crucifix and beads, which I still have. I promised to get him a good hat when I returned to the United States on leave.

Amal, my IT teacher at the GOIC, wanted to know about her home in Basra. I promised I'd find it if she gave me directions and a description.

I got proposals from and talked to all three sides (my company, the military, and the Iraqis). My salary took a big jump, to more than $18,000 a month. In the contracts, they billed to the government, my salary was listed at eleven times more than what I was actually paid. I understood the risk, so I let them work their own pricing structure and went to work on deliverables. Everybody had an agenda. My company wanted to keep billing, the Iraqis wanted autonomy, and the military wanted control and peace. I needed a workable plan to give everyone at least his top priority, if possible. The military lost total control but got peace and better intelligence reporting. The Iraqis got control of their network as much as they could (phones, servers, and PCs but not the satellite dish), and my company kept billing. It was the first contract to be completed with the Iraqi government since Saddam's defeat. It was three days before I returned to Basra, but I did my company a solid with the renewal, and all were pleased. I was sorry to leave the wonderful VIP trailer.

Return to Basra

The last photograph of Likka and her sister, who were shot just outside the front gate by their own uncle.

Basra had a major incident while I was gone. Two very nice local Iraqi sisters had worked at our laundry. Likka was the happy one, always loving a free candy bar and some light conversation. Her sister was nice but more serious. Likka was a little chubby, but her laugh was magical and her attitude was inspiring. The sister was thinner with a better figure and looks, but she didn't have the

Likka magnetism. Likka had been dating the head of the laundry, a black man who worked for KBR, also likeable. It was always a friendly atmosphere at the laundry. Her family was not pleased that she was dating a Western man and a non-Muslim. Likka and her sister were leaving work one Thursday in a taxi. Her uncle was waiting with an AK-47 and killed the driver and his nieces without batting an eye. Under Islamic law, the uncle was permitted to do this, but the sister or the driver had nothing to do with Likka's relationship. It happened just outside the gates, so local justice, not our laws, prevailed. It really made me think.

Likka's uncle waited outside the gate and then slaughtered her, her sister, and the taxi driver.

On the lighter side, the Iraqis in Basra were happy to see me. They tried hard to have me take their picture, because they knew I would print a copy for them. I was happy to do it, and they were really enthusiastic.

Camp construction workers were thrilled when I took their pictures. I made sure everyone got an 8 x 11 color copy.

I rode around with New Zealand security staff to check out the sights, and we stopped at Ur, one of the oldest cities in the world. Zagat was the main temple, and it afforded a nice view of the landscape. It's very close to where Abraham's home is believed to have been.

Zagat still rises from the ancient city of Ur in southwest Iraq.

I searched for Amal's home using her directions. Iraqis were not allowed to take map training, and with few street signs, directions were based on landmarks. I found her square water tower and took a picture of her home. She'd lost it in the Iran-Iraq War in the late 1980s. She was a Christian among Shiites, and when she returned after the fighting, the locals had moved in and made her leave.

Amal was heartbroken when she saw how her once-beautiful home had been trashed and ghettoized.

Iraqi tanks from the Desert Storm—era, destroyed and abandoned at the airport fence west of Basra.

In February 2004, we prepared for a special visitor. Security was high, because Prince Charles was coming for an inspection. He went first to the British troops area in his camouflage outfit and beret. When he visited the US embassy he changed to a sports coat. We were lined up from the road to the palace entrance. I was under the eaves at the outside corner of the palace, with my Iraqi help-desk guys and Franz. Everyone who was anyone was there. The British secret service kept trying to push me and the guys back, but I was bigger and held my ground. When the prince reached me, I introduced myself and said, "I bet it's nice to get away from home pressures for a while." (According to the tabloids, he had been fighting with the queen and the public about his relationship with Camilla.) He smiled, and I said, "Let me introduce you to my Iraqi help-desk staff." I introduced Dolfakar, Hamid, Basil, and the rest. Prince Charles was very pleased, and the CNN cameras and reporters surrounded us with great fervor. Charles wanted to know about Iraqi life with Saddam and after, how they felt, and the suggestions they had. He spent twenty minutes with us (much to the security men's unhappiness), and he got to relax for a few minutes. He then proceeded up the line at the insistence of a brigadier general, and he was inside the palace five minutes later.

Prince Charles, a very gracious and nice man, three months my junior.

Charles was very excited to meet my Iraqi help-desk staff.

I thought it wonderful that my guys were able to participate in a moment of history in their own country, but I was wrong. Unfortunately for them, the CNN broadcast was replayed on Al Jazeera, and my guys were scared stiff about the prospect of going home. I went to the British ambassador and got a special disposition for them to stay inside the fort for a week. I think that after that they felt special and grew really close to me.

After their interview with the prince and the reporters, my guys got timid.

It was time for a weekend getaway. DoD had an agreement with KBR, which provided free accommodations in Kuwait for US troops on R&R. It was a beautiful ocean-side hotel and had excellent food.

A Kuwait City breakfast. The view would have been
more resort-like without the oil tankers.

Kuwait seemed to have two faces. The people were friendly enough, but *wadj* (face) was everything. Just as American men in the 1950s always wore suits and porkpie hats, the Kuwaitis wore their "man dresses," called *dishdasha*, and headdresses. Many societal rules were in effect, such as no drinking or kissing even in the movies. But violence and smoking were permitted on screen. The average Kuwaiti family wore designer jeans at home and had a bar and satellite TV.

A person who was at least half Kuwaiti got a government stipend of $50,000 per year, and if he had an official job, it was tripled. The border guards were usually less than half Kuwaiti or Pakistani. Servants were tightly controlled and were from other countries like Sri Lanka, India, or the Philippines. In school, a Kuwaiti child always got 95 percent, but the others had to earn their grades. I felt this was a disservice to their youth, even though they automatically had an income.

Enjoying the view from Kuwait's famous landmark tower.

Me at the park. The Kuwait Towers are depicted on the country's money.

Our weekend Kuwait dalliance over we drove back over the border. It was almost Easter so Christians dress up for Easter and people everywhere love to party, so why not? We had eight golf carts to drive around the base and eight teams of four. Se2 and Franz were with two others from IT, dressed up as pirates. The different offices each registered a team, and each one got a golf cart. They were given treasure maps and had to find things around the site. I sat on a roof to watch the action, which ranged from balancing eggs on a knife to discovering actual hard boiled eggs. We came in second but the British ambassador's office won. (It had to be fixed.) Everyone seemed to have a great time. Craziness relieves stress.

Kat handled the local contractor money.

Bull (another contractor and my partner with the bar and movie theater) went with Kat to Baghdad to pick up cash and came back with skids of $100 bills in a Chinook chopper. There was more than $16 million in cash (160,000 hundred-dollar bills), and she signed for everything. Her area approved and paid all the Iraqi contractors in the British sector. She would stay at the palace for two weeks and then return to Germany for a week or so. She was from a very wealthy family; Bull was her favorite, and then Brad, both good sized Army contractors.

I was asked to pretend I was one of Congressman Talent's Missouri constituents.

Congressman Talent from Missouri came for a visit on a "fact finding" mission. Since he was from Missouri, I told him he was actually on a "show me" tour. I had spent time in Missouri with my best friend John, so the Basra heads lied and said I was one of his constituents. I played along and got a nice lunch with the congressman. We had croissants with beef, and I said we'd killed a mule in his honor. He was a personable and likeable man. Too bad there was only one guy from Missouri in Basra. Eight showed up for lunch, saying they were from Missouri, but at least I could talk extensively about his home state and hometown, Saint Joseph.

Italian tanks do not have treads, which makes no sense to me. Treads work better in the sand.

A visit to the Italian camps by Nasiriya was always fun. They served red wine and pasta and were very neat in appearance. They manufacture the Beretta 9 mm but carry Colt .45 automatics. As a whole, their attitude is positive and nonaggressive. Their network and satellite knowledge was poor so I was constantly repairing and adjusting components.

I had to go to the Italians' HQ to repair their switch system as one part of the network could not be accessed. It was the area controlled by the head enlisted man (the equivalent of our master sergeant), so I began the search for loose or broken cables. I backtracked to his switch, which was out in the hall on the floor by a desk. When the troops went into his office, they'd put their equipment on that desk and any extra went on the floor—on top of the switch, which was crushed by the weight. They did not have a spare, so I found a different working port and set him up.

The Italians were very proud of their captured Iraqi ordinance.

The next time I went there was at the behest of the Italian ambassador and Paola. They wanted to evacuate the staff and save their server data. I went with the British escort convoy, and the Italian camp was being mortared and rocketed from a nearby hospital roof. I completed my mission and retrieved their server but was amazed that no one was attacking the shooters. I looked through some binoculars from the satellite position and saw only four guys. The senior enlisted man was longtime military, so I discussed the counterattack with him while the server and administrative staff were being loaded on the convoy. I had to leave, but I think it worked and that he retook the hospital roof.

The insurgents mortared and rocketed us from the roof of Nasirya Hospital.

The Ashura ("*This day is well-known because of mourning for the martyrdom of Husayn ibn Ali, the grandson of Muhammad the third Shia Imam, along with members of his family and close friends at the Battle of Karbala in the year 61 AH (680 AD). Yazid I was in power then and wanted the Bay'ah (allegiance) of Husayn ibn Ali. A segment of Muslims believed Yazid was openly going against the teachings of Islam in public and changing the sunnah of Muhammad.*" reference from Wikiopedia) was on, and there was a big parade. The boys took off their shirts and whipped themselves until they were bloody. The Prophet Muhammad's grandson Hussein bin Ali had refused fealty to Yazid in the seventh century AD. He was beheaded in Karbala, and today that is the holiest site for Shiite Muslims. Saddam Hussein would not allow this parade to take place as he was a Sunni Muslim, and their beliefs are not the same. To this day the Sunni still attack the Shi'a sacred Karbala mosque.

View of Iran across the Tigris and Euphrates Rivers.

The Fijian guards at the front gate. The Gurkha contract
was over; Fijians came in $2,000 cheaper.

The coalition was winding down and would be finished by the end of June. The US Department of State (DoS) came in and changed the logo from Operation Iraqi Freedom to Operation Enduring Freedom. With DoS in charge, more Americans would come.

The help-desk staff with the new T-shirts I bought them. They loved them.

By the time I returned from Nasirya, the DoS had replaced the DoD, and the British had split the fort 70/30. They got the largest share and were responsible for military in the entire southern sector. The DoS put up its own dish, but on the ground in a stone field right outside the palace on the city side. I told their security people to put it on the roof with my dish; since the British were taking their dish, the DoS could even use the existing steel I-beam mounts. I argued that mortars and rockets were shot at us, and if they hit the gravel, the stones alone would wipe out the dish. They said they were worried about direct sniper fire from the rooftops outside the T-walls. T-walls are the taller concrete walls that surround the compound (J-wall is the shorter concrete wall used to stop cars). I told them Muslims can't use sights on weapons, so that's why they shoot so erratically. If you're hit from a wild shot, then inshallah (which is god willing). That was why their IEDs were so effective, because if they set one off nearby and it hit you—inshallah—it was not their fault. Three months later, when I returned to the United States for the first time in a year, they discovered my words to be true.

The SATCOM shed was next to the palace, with the dish on top. The DoS put its dish to the right of the generator.

August 10, 2004, 9:00 a.m.

The local militia fanatics were up in arms (literally) about the British military. We were supposed to be overrun, although I don't know why they would have leaked that to our "intelligence" guys. One of our IT guys, who lived there, also heard the rumor, but nothing happened. I was the only one in the office, and everyone outside was in helmets and flak jackets. I was never issued a helmet, and my "bullet proof" flak jacket was only level 2. I looked it up, and level 2 stops 9 mm and below. All the bad guys shot AK-47s, which it didn't stop. Only our guys had 9 mm so I was safe from friendly fire. All our guys had their guns on and were all set for the big attack. To our east, Iran was very close across the river, and many rockets and mortars came from there. I thought that strategically, unless they had artillery or air [power], it would be stupid to attack, especially in the daytime where our towers would easily destroy massed formations. The British had a couple of Centurion tanks that would also deter and ground attack.

A lot of ordinance went off for a couple of days, and our convoys stopped. The British got shot up pretty good, but I don't think anyone died. We only got water twice a day for an hour, so we had to manage bathing, shaving, flushing, etc. I sometimes abstained from cleansing, which meant no shower and I was scruffy. It was nice out, maybe 35°C (95°F), but I was sure the heat would be back up to 46°C (115°F) by 3:00 p.m. Choppers were everywhere in anticipation of the big strike. Al-Sadr (he is a radical cleric who kills and has his personal army, Sadr City next to Baghdad is named for his father a non-violent cleric) had vowed death to us, and that he would not surrender, and the fight would be to the death. I hoped he'd get his last wish. We got some RPGs, but they didn't hit inside the T-walls, except for a homemade grenade with nails at Tower 6. Before that, nothing made it into the compound, although a mortar round did hit next to the T-wall.

How long can you stay on alert? I guess I was too old and too much of a fatalist to be a model soldier. I'm sure that's why nineteen is the ideal age. I was twenty-three in Vietnam and had an attitude there. I had to attribute this crap to politics, not war. The CNN back in the States told one story and CNN Middle East told another. With the DoD gone from power, the big money was gone. DoS was budgeted and selfish. If I humped recordable CDs from Kuwait, they treated it like a deserved gift or made me fill out paperwork to get reimbursed. If I wanted to make copies on their machine, I had to pay a dollar a page. I hate carpetbaggers and administrators, and they have no use in combat.

August 13, 2004, 11:00 a.m.

Al-Sadr was wounded in Najaf, and some of his men came down to Basra to avoid the US action to the north. They carried their RPGs around on their shoulders to intimidate the people. Our Iraqi employees did not come into work and were still on lockdown. I had gone three days without a shower, and I'm getting ripe, and after a week, I even offended myself. There were ten-plus explosions last night, mostly local reprisals from their complex tribal system. I was the only one in an office that usually had eleven people, and the mullah was wailing on the loudspeaker with his chants calling for religious recognition. My company let five people go in the last two months, and my leave that had been scheduled six months earlier was in jeopardy. They already had paid for nonrefundable tickets to the States and back, so I was trying to get someone to cover me so I could go back to the States. I eventually got my leave in September.

August 18, 2004, 9:00 a.m.

Finally, two Iraqis came to work. They were terrified of Al-Sadr's men, who they said were drug users and criminals.

I hadn't heard much about the Olympics in Greece, other than they were not filling the seats. When the Iraqis won a soccer game, they fired off many bullets in celebration. Many people were hurt or killed in the celebratory shooting. We lost eight throughout the country. I didn't want to be an Iraqi. Even their good times were bad. It had been so quiet before Al-Sadr's troops got in town. Afterward, we heard explosions all the time—nothing in the compound here, but they were up to no good. SK was still trying to get my leave, but it was dependent on finding my replacement and the lockdown. Even the camp commander was having trouble moving to other sites.

I had been on a crash diet of throwing up, the runs, and only water; that had to stop. I was a wannabe bulimic (I think it was food poisoning). I had dinner and held it down, but I skipped breakfast. Two days with ass piss, vomit, and no ability to flush or wash with the water shortage (just live in your own stench) sucks! I think I finally earned my hardship pay. Even in Vietnam, I didn't get wounded. (I feel a bond with Geronimo, who never was hit.) I was going to be fifty-seven in eleven days, and I was the oldest guy there except for the Italian ambassador. I bribed a Pakistani in the kitchen for a bag of apples. My apples and water diet saved me from massive dehydration and cured the runs.

After the coalition broke up at the end of June 2004, our palace compound became American, with new rules and people. The Danes grew fewer and then nonexistent after someone published a picture of Mohammed in a cartoon back in Denmark. We lost all those great dairy products due to one religious faux pas.

We had young seals and CIA guys everywhere trying to get credit for a hostile action. They liked to network and play video games, so they called on me. I made a private network so they could pair up for *Halo* and other war games. We got three new, all-black, armor-plated Mercedes for some of these guys. Like the characters in their video games, they drove in formation with a lead vehicle, wingman, and a tail. They had very precise movements but unhinged locals with their rude driving.

A week later, they were in fleet formation, very quickly traversing Basra. The lead car went into a deep pit, the wingman followed very precisely, and the tail topped them off like a fancy armor-plated sandwich. The locals stared at the debacle as they got out of the cars and covered each other with their machine pistols. They immediately radioed camp for the armored bus and were "rescued" in about a half hour. They got back to the accident site an hour and a half later with reinforcements only to find two cars crunched and the good one (the one on top) removed by donkeys. One of the donkeys had crapped on the middle car while it was working. I told them to pick up the turds and take them to their lab for analysis. The top car was never found and the other two were shipped to Kuwait for repair. These guys were shipped out after spending ninety days total in country.

Soccer (football) is very popular here. The football pool is the big betting thing, and I took Greece for 2004 Olympics. I was ignorant about it, and Greece had never played soccer in the Olympics. Fortunately for me, they had this old goal keeper who was awesome, and they just won ugly. I made a tidy fortune on total luck. I had French legionnaires, Italians, and of course the

British cursing my Greeks. I told them it was a fix, because the Greeks were the home team. Thanks to my Greeks beating the "great" teams, the Iraqi team almost got a medal, and they were very proud. They went a long way and even though they just missed the bronze, it was remarkable considering the teams they were playing against.

Early champions of the Basra Bazoona Football League

Foreign service national (FSN) is the DoS term for a non-US citizen who works for the US embassy or government. I preferred to call them locals, because we were the foreigners. My personal contribution to the area (besides fostering friendship and bonding banter) was via sports. While in country, I cultivated an interest in football but by no means expertise. The Iraqis were embargoed from everything, thanks to us, and could not compete in anything or make international purchases. They had no grass or indoor sport facilities. In spite of this (and Uday's penchant for killing losers), they put together a soccer team for the Olympics. War-torn people need a positive thing to focus on, if they're going to grow. This was very uplifting in their time of despair and death.

I got balls, pumps, and a commitment from Carolina High School for used uniforms and shoes.

I counted ten soccer fields in Basra, so I decided with my own money and time to obtain a good ball for each field to encourage local play and future Olympians. I searched the Internet and found a site in Basra where I could get items delivered. I chose the Italian ball brand Puma, because it has a cat for the symbol and *bazoona* (cat) is one of my favorite Arabic words. The balls were coated with a durable surface so they would last longer on gravel play. One ball kept twenty-two players on the soccer field. I have a photograph of the first six (junior-size) T-shirts I sent to Basra and one from the Chicago Fire, the professional soccer team in my hometown. I obtained four more (full-size) T-shirts and four ball pumps with nozzles. It wouldn't save the world but hopefully would put a couple of Basra's children on the Olympic team in four or eight years, and maybe take some stress away and bring some enjoyment in a troubled place. These are good people here, and very few, if any, are the mad suicide bombers who get all the press.

Bull, my bar and movie-theater partner.

Bull (a fun-loving guy from Texas) and I decided the old bar had to go, so we pooled some money for liquor runs. BIAP was too far, so we went to the British port of entry, where they stored liquor rations in CONEXs. This is a larger trailer like a full size truck without the engine. They can be shipped by truck or boat. By that point, we knew all the security people and police who drove off compound and did convoys. We would ride along as "spare" gunners, holding machine guns or AK-47s. Thirty-two years after Vietnam I was still pretty good at shooting at moving or stationary targets with a machine gun in a moving vehicle. We got our startup stock and gave each of the drivers a case of beer for their efforts.

We had KBR put up a double trailer without rooms, but one had two bathrooms for our customers. They were connected by a roof and in-between we set up picnic tables on a concrete pad. The side with the bathrooms got the bar and refrigerators, and the other side was a meeting room and theater. KBR ordered a projector, and we acquired tables and chairs. I brought my microwave (one of two in the camp) and popcorn. Amazon shipped to APO addresses, so I ordered lots of movies. I paid for them myself and kept them afterward (starting my collection back home). I aired a different movie every night and printed flyers to put up in the mess hall every morning so people would know what was playing. Bull opened the bar at 8:00 p.m. There was seating for fifty, but usually ten to twelve showed up. When I showed *Cold Mountain*, however, all the seats were taken, and six more were standing. I took the microwave back to my office most nights, so my Iraqi staff could heat their meals.

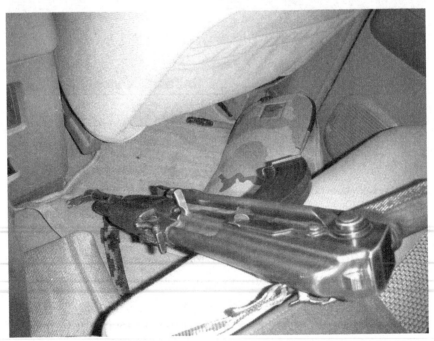

The AK-47 I used on the road, 2004–5; it had a nice fold-up stock for use in the car.

Two days before I returned from R&R stateside, we were hit. Our dish survived while the State Department's was compromised on the stones. "I told you so" doesn't matter, so I said nothing about my argument three months earlier. From then on, all the uploads had to go out my dish until they could get the seal team guys in to set one up for them. I placed port security on the lines I ran to them in the interim. My system wasn't NIPR or SIPR military-rated, but DoS did allow NIPR (not as secure as SIPR) to run on it temporarily out of desparation.

The hole that was made very close to our dish; notice the shadow.

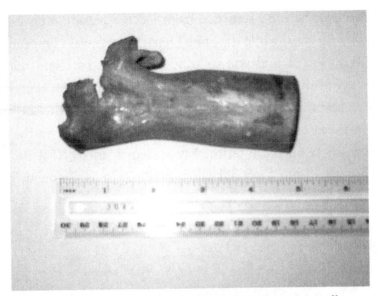

Fortunately, homemade shrapnel didn't fragment well.

Recreation seemed more important after the destruction cleanup, so I focused more on the new bar the Squealing Donkey and the attached movie theater. Amazon was awesome, delivering movies in only two or so weeks.

Bull and I liked the girls to take turns as bartenders.

Kuwait 2005

st assignment with T-O was to relieve IT at Port Shuaiba.
ed on SIPR for the first time, which is the military secret
ice network and not on the public Internet. NIPR is the
·y network with Internet access for the troops but has lots
rictions and security. Kuwait was a nonviolent area with
Islamic rules.

*Unused vehicles sat by the thousands in Kuwait; I
personally counted six hundred tanks.*

I bought Abu Jacob two hats at the Stetson factory in Saint Joseph, Missouri, when I was on R&R. They were pork-pie hats from the 1940s and 1950s. One was felt; the other had a brushed finish with a band and feather. I brought them back in a hatbox for him. Abu Jacob had jumped ship from the Iraqi navy around 1980 when Saddam first got in. He lived with a woman in Baltimore, who took him in and was in love. Saddam complained, and the United States extradited him to Iraq to his forced-marriage wife. She was Christian, and when returned he stayed with her until he died in 2008.

I couldn't get up to Baghdad to see him, but one of the guys was picking up a part there, so he took the hatbox for me. I knew how much Abu Jacob loved that style of hat, and he was disappointed he couldn't see me. Little did I know he only had three years to live. I'll bet he was buried in one of those hats.

*We were shot at with these rockets, which were set off with a
car battery, but after the first hit nothing happened.*

We took more rockets in early 2005. The insurgents set them up in tubes with electrical ignition from a car battery. Physics clearly was poorly taught, because after the first one or two went off, the others would get out of line from concussion. This made for a lot of misses and unnecessary dead or wounded civilians and livestock. For every one or two coalition forces they got, they killed a hundred civilians due to poor technology.

The British found our bar very attractive. Our darts, snacks, décor, and alcohol selection were considerably better than theirs. They also enjoyed our nightly movies. Unfortunately the British, Irish, and Australians loved to Taser each other when they were loaded (usually on the back of the neck). After closing, I would have to pick them out of the brush and get them into an electric cart to haul to the British side.

We started showing each other our scars in the Squealing Donkey, and I have a huge vertical belly scar from my Agent Orange operations. A cute, inebriated British junior officer was very interested and unbuckled her pants and mooned me, sans her knickers (panties). She demanded my attention and another drink, so we sat down at a table after she pulled up her britches. The ratio was ten men to one woman, so every guy kept close to her. Due to the Tasers and stripping, the British were banned from coming to our bar. There were guards at the T-wall, and the British could not visit without express permission. People needed an outlet, and we were it.

April 2005

In Basra, SK's contract ended. I'd negoti extensions, but we were bought out by a co received my full secret clearance the previ demand. I had hardly been home when I was Benning, Georgia, and another journey to and Balad, Iraq. T-O needed someone who w in hostile zones to set up equipment for FOBs bases) to receive communication via e-ma phones. I met Jim, my replacement on the but he was more of a cable puller than a net by a rocket and died that September.

I flew a lot with military troops and was usually the

My f
I wor
cleara
milita
of res
many

I was asked to police our guys on Internet porn usage and improper downloading. Life was micromanaged for the "good" of the men. I felt very hypocritical setting port security on what our guys could view. It turned out one sergeant was downloading porn for hours in the middle of the night when the bandwidth was least used. This kind of a witch hunt was counterproductive. I did as told and left my data scans but would not testify to support political finger-pointing.

Our "secret" mission was about sand. We were offloading sand from Egypt to make J- and T-wall concrete barriers. J is the long, half wall, and T is the tall, upright concrete wall. Apparently Kuwait's and Iraq's sand doesn't work for mixing concrete mix, so they import the correct granular type from Egypt. It reminded me of Samuel Taylor Coleridge's *Rhyme of the Ancient Mariner*:– "Water, water everywhere and nary a drop to drink." Kuwait and Iraq had so much sand everywhere, and yet none was useful for construction except as a sandbag filler.

The Kuwait Towers revolving restaurant. There were pictures of the Iraqi invasion and abuses on the floor below.

My three-week relief job in Kuwait ended, and I was directed to the Bagram base in Afghanistan to set up a dish and communication on the west-side FOB. By the time I'd learned all the good eating places—I even found a Popeye's Chicken and a Hard Rock Café—it was time to leave.

Afghanistan, 2005

From Kuwait, I had to take a C130 to Kyrgyzstan, then down to Kabul, Afghanistan. The plane had bad karma from the beginning. We waited in Kuwait for six hours as the C130 readied for takeoff. We finally took off and had to return in twenty minutes due to electrical problems. We were offloaded and waited for the repairs. We took off again after another four-hour wait.

A tough and noisy landing, blowing the tires grinding the wheels
and their stems off on the landing pavement to the belly doors.

The C130 is a sturdy plane and can take a lot of grief, which is why it is still used after sixty years of service. We began our descent to Kabul, and everything seemed okay despite the false starts. The second our wheels touched the runway, a vibration began. With deceleration, the tires collapsed on one side, and quickly the rubber was gone. There was a loud scraping noise as the wheel was ground down by the cement runway. The noise inside the fuselage was deafening, and one or more of the troops began convulsing and vomiting to everyone's dismay. The troops were very apprehensive and could not wait to disembark. I was the last off because I knew how safe the plane was. There was no gasoline smell, only vomit. My picture shows the belly doors for the gear almost touching the ground after the rubber, wheels, and stem had been ground off. I was very impressed with this plane once again and ended up working with the manufacturer, Lockheed Martin, a year later in Oman.

The wheel stem scarred the runway badly, and we stopped right where the two runways crossed, so no one in a fixed wing could land until our plane was removed. I stayed around and took some pictures and then followed the troops to the terminal. Inside, there were stores and a bar, so the troops were enthused. They were stressed out and never fired a shot. A colonel came by and asked if anyone wanted a ride to Bagram for there wouldn't be another plane for a day or so. I was the only volunteer.

It turned out he was the Bagram base commander, and we just had four Humvees—unarmored, but green, not tan like in Iraq and Kuwait. It was nice to meet someone closer to my age and chat about the war and the past. We looked out and saw smoke stacks in the country, and they were quite high, maybe in excess of five stories for a city boy and sixty feet for a country lad. They looked like mini-factories, and there were always two together. The colonel told me they were for brick manufacturing, and they were so tall for the ventilation draft. We were in a plateau but were surrounded by mountains.

*The road from Kabul to Bagram. The commander invited
me to take his Humvee convoy back to the base.*

Notice in the photograph the circular (concertina) barbed-wire fencing, which was installed to protect travelers. It kept people away from the minefields that plagued the country. Cows, kids, and others were always blowing up. Afghanistan had more landmines than anywhere else. It was estimated that if all the minesweepers went there, it would take ten years to remove all the mines.

Bagram

Nestled in a mountain plateau, the area is quite striking. Larger planes had to fly in a circle when taking off to clear the mountains. It was dry, but not as hot as Iraq.

Bagram airport surrounded by mountains.

After settling in, I explored the camp. It was pretty much a strip camp, all built around one road called Disney. There were some gravel side roads, but Disney was the heart of everything.

Walking on Disney. There was a shuttle, but it was easier to walk

I didn't see the greeting sign in the airport until I had been there a week, as I had driven in with the colonel. This was a military terminal and not nearly as lavish and well stocked as Kabul's airport.

The greeting at the Bagram airport.

The Polish troops had their own area. They were a fun loving lot, and when I had an interpreter or did my charades, we got along great.

The Afghan Polish unit—a fun group and big drinkers.

The main IT office was on Disney, and I often visited there to coordinate with the contractors and troops out at the western edge of camp. They were over a mile apart, so an alligator (which was similar to a golf cart) was faster when I had to transport parts.

A week after I arrived, our IT staff took a big hit. Their chopper was hit and nine died from a direct RPG right inside the door as they were flying through the pass. Two survived, and we had a very somber funeral march down Disney lane the main street in Bagram.

I bounced between IT and the new construction area, west of camp

This was my primary work, setting up a dish and communications for the newly developed part of Bagram. We had a laptop program in the CONEX; the dish was left on to aid our dish shot. An inch off here is over a mile in space, and we'd have missed our satellite bounce that allowed us to hook up phone and Internet. My pickup router was my link to all local phone and Internet sources. Servers, phone boxes, and eventually individual personal computers originated in this CONEX. The other guys were satellite guys, and I was the server and router expert. This was an excellent learning experience. I used the skills learned there many times during the next four years.

The dish on the west side of Bagram on a CONEX.

I shared my living quarters with five others. The showers and toilets were three blocks away, but we had some hot water and the toilets flushed.

Too many people bunked in this small place.

I flew to Balad, north of Baghdad and by Tikrit, for my new company. I left the Afghanistan hills forever. It was not a hospitable place, and death was always hanging over everyone's head. There was little infrastructure there and nothing of value in resources, except maybe a cash poppy crop. The people had been at war for far too long.

I left Afghanistan behind.

Balad and Tikrit

I stopped in Baghdad and caught up with acquaintances and then flew on a flying boxcar to Balad. We only flew seven hundred feet in the air, so I sat on my flak jacket.

Army plane for transportation of personnel and equipment.

The flying boxcar was the army's workhorse and carried our satellite dish components, servers, and general components between FOBs. Camp Victory, between BIAP and Baghdad proper, was our main supply base. Al Asad was the marines' main base, and we installed units there also.

In al Asad they had us install on the back of a truck. It was a contractor's truck, and after we left, they moved the truck and then complained that their communications were not working. I had to do it again, but on a CONEX set on the ground.

I know how hard it is to line up the shot for the dish, but this just asked for trouble.

On the way back to Balad, I saw this desert picture of untilled land that obviously had been irrigated at one time. I inquired about it. Apparently it had been a beautiful farm, but the valves in the pumps gave out, and no one had spare parts.

There were no spare parts so this farm returned to desert.

I preferred not to wear military clothing when I was working near Iraqis, but wore whatever the job required. Most the deaths caused by insurgents was due fragments from IEDs or exploding cars. A helmet and flak jacket was very unlikely to save a life.

Before a mission in the flying boxcar I was outfitted like this: lots of extra clothing and protection for no real purpose

The streets were full of mayhem and destruction. Fires would break out from gasoline explosions, and many innocent bystanders were fragged by IED shrapnel. The police in Iraq were the bravest of all and paid a heavy price as they were targeted the most.

His car struck, the brave Iraqi policeman walked down the street to assist the victims of s fire, caused by a combination of poor parts, poor grounding, and overloading. Many Americans do not understand the difference between 220v DC and 110v AC. Adapters, step-downs and extension cords take their toll, and the trailers and their occupants pay way too often.

Evidence of the poor electrical setup in Balad,
due to ignorance and stupidity.

In Balad, because we were in the heart of Sunni territory, the funding came through for our camp auto-phalanx. If we received incoming rockets or mortars, shots would be fired by the phalanx to remove the threat. It was more than 95 percent effective. Tikrit had been Saddam's hometown and power base, so we constantly patrolled there. I enjoyed traveling and setting up new areas for contractors or helping soldiers. T-O was not the people company that SK was, so in the fall of 2005 they decided I should just support one contractor for big dollars in Balad and stay put. I disagreed, and we parted company before the year was out.

Oman, 2006-7

I decided combat was the wrong way to proceed at my age (fifty-nine), so I applied at Lockheed-Martin. I had an MBA, Novell certification, CISCO certification, and a Microsoft MCSE. I had worked for General Electric before the war and had a valid secret clearance. Lockheed Martin didn't nearly pay as well by any means, but they set me up as a number two guy behind an ex-SK SATCOM lead in Thumrait, Oman, and I wouldn't be shot at anymore. I was in demand and could travel immediately. Corporations couldn't bill their clients (the navy, DoD, or air force contracts) until I got in country, so the ability to travel there was always a priority.

Oman is on the south side of the Saudi peninsula and is straight across from Iran at the Gulf of Hormuz. I flew there through Amsterdam, Istanbul, and Muscat. After preliminary shots and tests—the Omanis were very concerned about AIDS, so everyone who entered had to be tested—I proceeded to Salalah, one thousand kilometers west, almost on the Yemen border. I had learned well by this time to get everything for a year to fit into two wheeled suitcases. From Salalah, I could get to Dubai almost as quickly as I could get to Muscat.

Dubai is very wealthy and was not at war, so
most items could be purchased there.

For much of my time, I volunteered for whatever work was available to get the hang of the operation. First I did an "as is" and found all the inventory, switches, servers, PCs, parts, and routers. There were a huge amount of CISCO switches with red stickers on them. These were used for the secret military network and did not touch the public Internet. Everything had to be wiped from them before they could be shipped back. Apparently all the previous analysts couldn't figure it out. Even the IT heads were dumbfounded. I had enough parts to fill a couple of huge crates that measured six feet by six feet by twelve feet, more than 860 cubic feet of space.

I wiped them all clean, reloaded with a CISCO operating system, and called the Saint Louis–area airbase to pick them up. It was going to take a couple of weeks, so I stripped the older computer of usable RAM and working hard drives, keyboards, and mice. I threw them and the broken monitors and CPUs in three other boxes, so I had five crates to ship when the new equipment arrived from the States. I cleaned the storage tent and cabinets and loaded up only my good spares. I did a complete inventory of servers and all the rest and discovered the poor wire work that was crimping the computer ends and made wires hang everywhere. When I submitted all the paperwork from my "free" time, the bosses, my company and the client (the US Air Force) were extremely pleased with the new organization and quality assurance.

Thumrait is an airbase in northwest Oman, and the British have Jaguar jet fighters there to aid the Omanis against Yemen. Yellow cake uranium had been imported into Iran, and the fear of nuclear war was real. Oman was slated to ramp up with troops and planes if something was happened. I had to have fifty-plus servers ready and four hundred personal computers tested and ready to roll out with all the latest software and access. Good thing I'd shipped all the old hardware out.

It was strange to build a network that had no users, just switches in various areas—well covered because of the sand—ready to sync up when called on. All the new personal computers and laptops had to be ready to go and inventoried with software for a battle environment. I quickly had eleven users, counting our office, a medical unit that sent pictures to Cleveland and a Briton who got special permission. We usually were the only ones to use the SIPR, to encode and transition pilots (not in uniform) to communicate with the home brass.

Every day (a ten to twelve hour shift with a ninety-kilometer drive each way) was grinding, so schedules were staggered into night and day shifts. We were authorized to have six staff, but usually four or five of us ran the place. When we were fully staffed, with no one on mission or vacation, it was very comfortable and almost like stateside. Usually the guys would honky-tonk it locally or take a short trip to Muscat or Dubai. Oman had bars that were considerably more open and off-sale liquor. It was also nice that most everyone could speak some English.

Oman is a Sultanate, which is similar to a kingdom. People there were friendly and very honest. You could leave your car open and the keys in it, and it wouldn't be disturbed. They had no auto insurance and if you had a dent or rust thru you would be stopped by the police. You got a warning ticket and had so many days to get the car fixed. If not, your car was immediately impounded and you walked. I went to the Toyota dealer and there were literally many hundreds of cars waiting to be fixed in a giant warehouse behind the dealership.

I usually had one day a week off, while others took two and quickly slotted their vacations when we had enough personnel. Terry was the site lead and dish man, an ex-SK guy who had move to T-O, which was being bought out by DS. We had a nice three-meter dish, and once it was set there was little for him to do. He was married to a Filipino woman who was curvy and cute. She spent most of her time in the Philippines, but he did get a cottage to himself. They had bought a business together—his money, her family were employees—and then she divorced him. Under Filipino law, an American can't own property in the Philippines, only a citizen can. She took his retirement investment and the business for herself and her family. He was crushed and came back from a visit there as a recluse and a drunk. I felt bad but life goes on, and after a month of covering for him, I had a chat with him, and he started to come back. He started dating another Filipino woman who lived in Salalah, but he was never the same while I was there.

Dave #3 was from Texas and married to a Filipino woman whom he suspected was cheating on him, but he loved his sixteen-year-old daughter, who drove his BMW while he was overseas. He spoiled her but hated dealing with the wife, who wouldn't divorce him. I mentored Dave #3 on CISCO and servers, and he eventually got a job as the IT guy on a navy contract.

Sammy lived in a cottage with a Filipino woman, Christine, whom I paid to clean my cottage. Sammy wasn't married, but Christine was always pushing him toward the altar. There was a Filipino community in downtown Salalah; he would drop her off to gamble and talk smack about marriage. She then started a full-court press on a diamond ring so she could hold her head up in the community. She told me she would introduce me to her friend who was coming from the Philippines.

Frank was married to a Turkish woman, who I thought was attractive and pleasant, but I never spent a lot of time with her and neither did Frank. She was always going back to Turkey or visiting his parents in the States. The marriage seemed to work for both participants.

Three of the guys had totaled their SUVs when they hit cattle on the drive to work. Terry had one, and the other five of us shared two. Terry came late and left early so he wasn't much help with transportation. Unless you're good at driving in fog, it's a dangerous drive from Thumrait to Salalah. Unfortunately the other drivers kept trashing the SUVs into perfectly good cattle. I was also amazed that the Omanis would cross a road with black cattle at dusk or dawn.

Even if you bribed the Omanis, it still took two to three weeks to get your vehicle back. The other guys told me how horrible the system was, and we had no right of appeal. One day, it was my turn in the bucket. I was making a left turn to visit Sheba's Palace east of Salalah. I was stopped, waiting for a guy coming toward me, and after he passed I began to turn left. Another guy came flying by on the left side, trying to pass while I was making the turn. He spoke no English. His wife's brother was the local magistrate. Fortunately, the local police chief spoke English pretty well. I explained the accident with a box of paper clips and a large eraser. I'd called Terry, and he said, "Get out of there. No one wins. Let Lockheed Martin take care of it." That didn't sit well with me, and I stayed and explained my position. I found out later that the guy who hit me had had four accidents in the last year, all his fault.

A week later I showed up in court. Once again, Terry said he'd been there for years, and no one ever won. I showed up with an interpreter, and I won. The magistrate begged for mercy for his sister's husband. I said the only thing I was worried about was three weeks without the SUV. He got me into Toyota that was two years older to drive and got my car back in a week, so I dropped the charges. Nobody at work or headquarters could believe I'd won, got the car fixed so quickly, and got a free rental too. I told them it was the principle of the thing.

Thanksgiving had passed, and it was getting on toward Christmas season. I set up a port for medical and decided I needed one for me. I secured one high and used port 80 (Internet) for me on one computer so it wouldn't influence military NIPR. I had to put in extra hours because all the guys except Terry and me were going home for Christmas. I took nights and Terry took days, and Frank worked some too. I got on eHarmony in my spare time and met the woman of my dreams. Life radically changed for me and so did my focus.

I saw her profile and responded three days after her sixtieth birthday, the first week in December 2006. I had raised three children by myself, and so had she. Her profile was very honest and straightforward, with no games. Her picture almost reminded me of Mighty Mouse's girlfriend, and she had a smile that would brighten any room. I quickly answered all the required questions to rush to where we could exchange e-mails. I couldn't wait to respond to her e-mails and sent extra ones all the time because I couldn't wait for her to respond when I wanted to tell her something. I looked back later and realized that I'd written more than six hundred e-mails in six weeks. I had my son mail her a webcam so we could talk face to face. It turned out I was twenty-eighth on her list, and she was into classical musicians and maestros.

She was on eHarmony because her daughter (who resided in Oregon) had found a couple of guys that way, so she bought her mom thirty days of time for fun on her birthday. I think she did it as a joke because her mom was sixty. The future Mrs. Tenacity took it in stride and decided to pursue it. She translated her vitals into English and finished all the required questions. I had put no limit on distance, and neither did she. I was in Salalah, Oman, and she was in Cuiaba, Brazil. We matched up, but she had twenty-seven others in front of me. The picture I put in was my newest, but I'd been tired when it was taken in South Carolina. You couldn't see my hands as I was holding luggage and was slightly stooped forward. She thought I was a paraplegic Mexican and wanted little to do with me as she pursued her maestros. Her daughter, Martha, told her to write me and helped with the translation. The others would write her once and wait a day or two for her answer and not appear too eager. I liked her honesty and wrote her often and the more I got to know her the more I wrote. I sent her flowers but she never got them, and she gave me her number, but it was the wrong area code.

I felt like a bear at a honey tree, and when I reached into the hole I didn't know if there would be something sweet or bee stings. I knew she was the one, but she didn't yet. I looked at her as a woman, not a pianist, opera singer, or conductor. My competition didn't matter, so despite nine thousand miles of distance and culture and language differences I pressed on. She got the webcam my son mailed her and just in time, because she was retiring and moving near her oldest son in Sao Paulo. I finally got her right number and called her, but my Portuguese and her English were terrible. She could only "heh, heh, heh" but I could chat with her on the computer while she translated my text. She could read and write some but not speak much. She had been in classical music her whole life and sang in German, French, English, Italian, and Brazilian Portuguese. She conducted for Pope John Paul in Brazil and the Eastern patriarch a few months later. We began to communicate more and more and did not waste words, because translation is work, and we were getting serious. Martha called me Speedy Gonzales when I got Mrs. Tenacity to agree to meet me.

I asked her to meet me in Portugal, because she spoke the language, but to my surprise and delight she wanted to visit Oman. She figured if she was going to do this, she'd give it a good chance, not just a quick vacation. She sold all her stuff, and I sent her a ticket. The future Mrs. Tenacity didn't tell anyone about eHarmony—cyber dating was culturally inappropriate in Brazil at that time—and told her friends that I was one of Martha's teachers. When I told my friends that I'd sent her a ticket to Oman, everyone thought I was crazy, that she'd rip me off and sell the ticket. I wasn't worried and if I was fooled like that, it would be the cheapest breakup.

You never know how it will be with physical chemistry until you actually meet, but it's a grand leap of faith for both of you to try. I finally met her on January 22, 2007, at the Muscat airport. At first, I was worried because I didn't see her get off the flight with the other passengers. It turned out she had lost her baggage, and she was really worried about her shoes. The only thing she had was her electric keyboard, her purse, and the clothes on her back. She was very upset. I ran a check and the baggage had gone to Dubai by mistake and would follow us to Salalah in a couple of days. I told her it was my fault and that I'd bribed the baggage people to lose her luggage so she'd be at my mercy. That softened her up, and I explained what would really happen, and we began our magical physical relationship. The next day we flew to Salalah and her new home.

My love, Mrs. Tenacity, in the bushes by our cottage in Salalah in early 2007.

We had spoken on the phone/Internet for twelve hours, written hundreds of e-mails, and the physical part was just a natural progression. As I got to know her in the biblical and personal sense, a natural intimacy developed between us. Each day got better and after a while it started to seem like we'd always belonged together. Her sex appeal had awakened my basic love instincts. The Brazilian fire burned all remembrances of former women from my past. She became exclusive in my life like she was always in it. I even suggested she write a book *Sex over Sixty* in Brazilian Portuguese. Without even knowing it I was becoming a part of an Us, no longer just me and her.

This was shortly after Mrs. Tenacity arrived; the camels came down from the nearby hills.

Learning every little thing about each other became a full-time pleasure. I began planning around us, not just around work. We took country trips to see ruins and sights, such as Job's Tomb, a popular Arab tourist site, as were most oasis stops. We stopped at a banana grove along the coast road. I picked a huge bunch of fruit and the guy was preparing to charge me and I said, "Do you know the Chiquita Banana song?" He had never heard of it. His fellow entrepreneurs were also curious so I said, "If I sing you the song will I get a discount?" and they agreed and all got closer. I began, "I'm Chiquita Banana and I'm here to say, 'Eat a Banana every day!'(Sung to the tune of the famous commercial sashaying like Carmen Miranda) They laughed and absolutely loved it and gave us the bananas for free. We explored together and enjoyed life.

Our home and SUV in Salalah, 2007.

Mrs. Tenacity was impressed that when she went to the pool or workout Gym all the men would leave but when caught walking alone by the police she was taken to jail and had to wait until I came home to punish her for violating protocol. Women cannot walk alone. She was equally surprised when in the public market men would roll out a blanket filled with guns and sell them on the street. Also young burka clad women in Lulu's four story market were very curious about her skin, tiny clothes and shoulders. She was equally curious about their hand paintings and tattoos.

*East of Salalah, not far from Sheba's Palace, whose queen
the Omanis disavow, saying she was Yemeni.*

Oman—and to a lesser extent India, Yemen, and Somalia—
have been a part of the frankincense trade for five thousand years.
Frankincense comes from a hardy tree that attaches itself to rock
and grows in harsh climates. To get it out, the tree is sliced so it can
release its resin. You can get three crops out of a good tree. Oman
has the best, "white," translucent, and finest quality frankincense,
which can only be obtained on the third cutting. The white can
be eaten or burned and has a myriad of health benefits. It is
mentioned in the Hebrew Bible and in the Gospel according to
Matthew. Frankincense was worth more than gold in Jesus's time,
because when burned around a newborn (especially in a stable), it
cleared the air of bugs and germs.

The frankincense tree provided baby Jesus with protection.

Oman is very dry, like Saudi Arabia, but it is very special by Salalah in the state of Dhofar. A miraculous event occurs called a *kareef,* which is like a monsoon but with far less water and lots of fog. It's why this is the best climate for frankincense. Arabs visit from many other countries to enjoy the phenomenon. Once, I was driving to work in the fog for my nightshift, and I saw three sets of lights coming toward me. They were expensive white Lexus SUVs, and when the third one passed, something hit my side-view mirror. It was a child who was hanging out of the car to enjoy the mist. Fortunately, he wasn't hurt, and my mirror had a release on it, so it wasn't broken either. I went on to work, and on the way home in the early morning, I saw all three Lexus SUVs smashed into the mountain on the way to Salalah. Water and exhaust oil made the road slippery for the tourists, who probably had driven only on sandy roads. I don't know how they all fared, but their vehicles were out of commission for a while.

When it rains on hot, dry, powdery sand, the ground seems to boil. One inch of rain can kill idiots driving in the dry gullies called *wadis*. The rain rapidly rolls down the slopes, and in the dry *wadi* a flash flood of force happens. The local rich kids in Salalah and even Muscat love to *wadi* bash with their expensive Mercedes, BMWs, and Lexus SUVs. During Cyclone Gonu in 2007, eighteen beautiful SUVs were totaled. Many still had rich kids in them, upside down and drowned. In the Arab Sea, they are called cyclones; in the Pacific, they are typhoons; and in the Atlantic, they are hurricanes. Gonu was only between a tropical storm and category one hurricane, and yet it was a big surprise to many of the younger generation.

If Mrs. Tenacity had been in Oman during Cyclone Gonu she'd have had to swim for her life.

I got a terrible ear ache and went to an Oman doctor. It had swollen shut and was throbbing terribly. His nurse gave me a shot and he prescribed drugs for me. I paid them and when I got the prescription filled I noticed he was not an ear doctor but was a dentist. Apparently that's enough education to certify you in whatever you wish to pursue.

I took the Mrs. Tenacity to work one day, and we had breakfast in the NCO mess hall.

We went to the Crown Plaza Salalah for a great breakfast buffet every Sunday. We got to know the staff and the head waiter took a shine to my wife. He would bring her a silver gravy boat full of fresh liquid chocolate for her coffee and pancakes. She absolutely loved it. All their food was fresh cut and well prepared with local and international cuisine.

Farms by the Salalah–Thumrait road.

Mrs. Tenacity modeling near the Salalah Oasis Club anchor.

The front entrance of the Oasis Club. One year later Captain Phillips sailed out on his fateful journey from the building next door. The Maersk shipping line's offices were there, and I'm sure Captain Phillips drank and ate at the British owned club.

My love, Mrs. Tenacity, never resisted and agreed to marriage, so we planned to get hitched in Thailand. It is very difficult to get a Christian wedding in Muslim Oman. In March 2007, we headed to Thailand for Saint Patrick's Day. We flew on Oman Air. Interestingly, if an Arab female is seated next to a Westerner, she can ask to be moved or for you to be moved. Arab women do not wish to be soiled by your corruption. Ordinarily I didn't care, but I observed deliberate abuse.

There are different cultural rules when flying in Oman.

Omani women hang out together at the airport in small packs, waiting for an opportunity. They observe Westerners, and one buys a ticket when she sees one or two Westerners buy a reserved seat ticket. The rest of the pack buy standby tickets (which are much cheaper) while the reserved ticket buyer gets a seat next to the Westerner. Once on board, the reserved-seat woman in a burka complains to the stewardess because she's been seated by a Westerner and asks for the other passenger to be moved elsewhere. Then her friends in standby rush up from the back to fill the seats. Our flight to Thailand was semifull, and my fiancée had a window seat so she could see the countryside. When the stewardess came to ask me to move I said, "No, I paid for this seat." The rest of the pack in the back had been all set to move into their new digs, but they were rebuffed. The woman next to me tried again, and she did get the guy across the aisle to move, and the pack moved up. Interestingly, the one with the reserve seat didn't move from her aisle seat and the soiled Westerner. On a short trip to Muscat, I wouldn't really have cared, but it was the principle more than anything else.

Burka-wearing predators on standby.

Thailand, 2007

We flew across the Arab Sea and over India, the Bay of Bengal, and Myanmar (Burma). Finally, we reached Bangkok, Thailand. I was the only American on the flight, and Mrs. Tenacity was the only Brazilian. I went to the US embassy and completed all my paperwork quickly. My Mrs. Tenacity had more paperwork and proof requirements than I did, but the Brazilian embassy staff wanted more than documents. They wanted Brazilian citizens to vouch for her. Now the staff there numbered about six, and there were no customers but us. We asked if we could send someone in Brazil to the government building in Brazil or send a fax directly to them. They said no, only originals. It was the first time I saw my love cry. She couldn't believe her own people would sabotage her wedding.

We had already ordered our rings, so when they came we put them on anyway. We went to a jewelry store/manufacturing place. It was guarded by two armored cars, machine guns, and well-armed troops. It was surrounded by concertina wire and had four hundred workers inside. It was huge and wealthy inside, where gold and jewels were processed and polished. We picked a seven-plus-carat sapphire with a diamond surround and a custom gold clasp that fit a large, solid, gold rope chain. We were out of there in an hour with our custom necklace.

We only had a week off, so we decided to finish the honeymoon. We went sightseeing on the river and visited many different restaurants.

Great sights on the river in Bangkok.

We got a cabbie to go to the river market two hours outside of town. We rode around in the boats with the long propeller at the back used for steering. We rode around to the shops, and Mrs. Tenacity got out to try on clothes. She found several nice outfits. Peddlers would float up to you with fresh pineapple, cut like a Christmas tree on a stick. They were quite cool and tasty.

We drove forty-five minutes deep into the jungle and went elephant riding. They are very gentle, and we had no trouble steering or with charging (going very fast). In the water, the elephant swam gracefully with her trunk up high. To go faster, we squeezed our legs, but if we relaxed too much and our knees touched the back of her ears, she swatted our legs hard with the same ears. At the ride's end, we bought a bunch of bananas and fed her. It was a nice time.

This was splendid, riding on a pachyderm in the jungle.

Oman Return Late March 2007

After our return, vacation over, we decided to try for a Christian marriage in a Muslim country. The paperwork and effort was prodigious. We first went to the gulag, where they kept all the non-Islamic religions together behind unmarked walls. Inside it was fine, as evidenced by the photograph of the pastor's home. He was Swiss with a wife and two boys, a nice kid but very worried about his position. He told us about his required marriage classes and the government paperwork. We went to the classes but had to laugh; after all, I was almost sixty, and Mrs. Tenacity already was. We both had been married before and each had three kids. But we were trying to accommodate this nice young man.

The pastor's home in the Omani gulag.

Even though we completed the classes and did the paperwork, the Swiss pastor was too afraid to ask his Salalah bosses for permission. We got a hold of the country boss, Pastor Ed in Muscat. He was great and understood the Omani thought process and got along well with them. We had to travel to Muscat twice more to do paperwork and set everything up. As in Thailand, we had to go to the embassy and many other Omani government buildings with our passports and Omani IDs. I had an Omani driver's license, and we both had two-year visas. We had to show shot cards and get medical exams and signatures or stamps from many different agencies. The US embassy would not marry us but gave me the necessary paper trail to accomplish an Arab ceremony. After I did that and got it stamped at all these offices, we could get married and then get the US blessing and marriage certification. Finally, we were ready for the ceremony.

We finally were married on April 27, 2007, by Pastor Ed.

The church's janitor and his wife kindly consented to be our witnesses.

Pastor Ed was a wonderful church person and human being. He was calm and collected. It was a simple ceremony in a simple church, but the feeling was so strong. I just stared into my bride's eyes, lost in the moment and grateful to have finally achieved what had seemed impossible. The love just beamed off our bodies as we said the words. I had never seen or felt anything like this before in my sixty years of existence. This wonderful woman had filled so many voids in my life, and now we were symbolically and spiritually united. A new entity was created that day, and we now had a third person to nurture officially—one called us.

After we completed the nuptials, it was off to the government agencies for more stamps (two are on the front of our certificate) and more fees. Our time ran out, and one man had sabotaged our final approval before we could submit it to US embassy staff, so they could work on their pre-requirements for my wife's US entry and citizenship track. He was the minister of notary, an official witness of signatures and authentication. He wanted Pastor Ed and the wedding witnesses in his office before he would stamp the certificate and charge the exorbitant fee. This was a power thing, and he implied that I'd never get his approval at all. I called Pastor Ed, and he told me to visit a vizier who was second only to Sultan Qaboos. I had to leave him with our passports, our stamped original marriage certificate, and a DHL envelope addressed to us in Salalah. I was nervous about entrusting these documents, but once again a leap of faith prevailed. The certificate was approved, and we received our documents in the DHL envelope within a week.

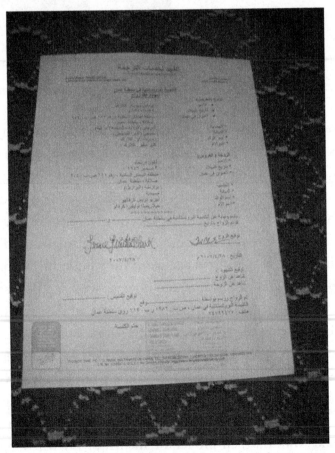

The first step on Mrs. Tenacity's journey to eventual US citizenship.

In two weeks, we were back in Muscat, getting our documents ready for the US embassy now that we had our final stamp from the vizier. We received a new myriad of paperwork and had to jump through hoops in order to get Mrs. Tenacity to the United States.

Before the US embassy processed our paperwork, we had to pay for the translations and get them certified.

The Ministry of Finance, one of the many government
agencies in Muscat that rarely opened for business.

My contract was up in August, and we thought we would never complete the American requirements. The basic form was $4,000 to start, and there were many more, each costing many dollars. This required considerable tenacity, but we were in love so we took it in stride and did some sightseeing and shopping as long as we were in Muscat.

The coastline in Muscat is very rocky, but there are still some nice beaches.

Mrs. Tenacity scares the locals in a Muscat shopping mall.

In the evening, we met some nice Irish teachers at a wonderful Indian restaurant. We had some drinks, an excellent dinner, and good conversation.

Good folks from Ireland.

My home office could not get a replacement by August 1, so I said we would stay on. I figured we would go back to Muscat and get her physical, chest x-rays, and the rest to complete as much as we could for the US immigration department. I got the approval from the embassy on our marriage, and we automatically won the immigration lottery under the legitimate marriage to a current citizen provision. I kept up with the forms, exams, and proof of financial responsibility for Mrs. Tenacity.

Our taxi driver said that a couple hours out of the city, there was a museum in a fort. We both enjoyed the experience and played with thousand-year-old objects. I had never been to a museum where you could use all the stuff as it had been used originally. Very few people and tourists are aware of this place, but I felt very special touching the past.

This desert fort outside Muscat houses an unusual museum.

I actually got to play with thousand-year-old weapons.

Mrs. Tenacity got to play with thousand-year-old utensils.

The rifles were from the early 1900s; most had been used in WWI.

On our next visit, we went to an oasis where the headwaters were for the main river. People washed clothes in a clear spring, and we were definitely the only Westerners within fifty miles.

The water was very nice, and the poor villagers washed clothes in the stream.

Once we had completed most of our embassy work, we returned to Salalah. Mrs. Tenacity sold her keyboard to our landlord, and I barbequed on the grill in our backyard. Our time in Oman was growing short.

Cooking spuds and steak in my Bagram T-shirt.

Mrs. Tenacity surprised me on my sixtieth birthday. She melted chocolate scraped off Kit Kat bars to make frosting. She used pancakes for the cake, toilet paper and magic marker for the banner, and it was a special moment far from home. Around Labor Day we moved to a hotel in Muscat and waited for Mrs. Tenacity's formal immigration paperwork.

My sixtieth birthday, August 29, 2007.

We got home in the early fall and enjoyed a family get-together. Everyone met each other.

My three kids and granddaughter with Mrs. Tenacity's daughter. Left to right: Bob, Cristen, little Cristen, Ivone, me, Martha, and Tom.

Mrs. Tenacity and I hung around through Christmas. Then in early spring, I decided to do one more combat tour while she took ESL(English as a Second Language) classes. I took her to Southern Arizona while I trained for the biometric automated toolset (BAT) at Fort Huachuca. We were gone a month. and then I had to leave my love for a year. I had barely known her a year, and in April 2008 we had our first anniversary. I did not want the separation but knew it was best for financial reasons, and it would give her time to adapt on her own with honest help from my son, Bob.

Iraq, 2008–9

I had come in second to a boy in his twenties, but he decided not to go, and my clearance and background got me the job. After BAT training, I had to be able to retina scan, fingerprint, and create ID cards in a hostile environment. The data had to be uploaded to Baghdad and the FBI for analysis. I had to be able to train marines in the field to operate the equipment; help set up choke points for traffic; and repair, replace, download, and upload data in a very dirty environment.

I was required to go through chemical training for the third time at Fort Benning; then I was ready for South Carolina. I was on a navy contract and would be embedded with the marines. I preferred moving to sitting in combat, so they suited me fine. I received additional training about antiterrorism, captivity, and the like. I found it pretty much useless. Teaching people Arab words would have been more useful. I got a tooth filled and the rest cleaned. It would be a year before I saw a real dentist again.

Fallujah

*In my new hat; written in Arabic, the front
said Tom, and the back said infidel.*

I went into a base in Kuwait, and three days later I was flying a C130 into TQ(Al-Taqaddum) and the next day into Fallujah. There, I trained for specific applications related to the current operations. They then assigned me to the Third Recon Marines Division, and I was the only BAT guy with them. I trained two guys who were pretty clueless, but after a week of training, they were ready to enter data, search fingerprints, and scan retinas. One retina scan holds more positive identification than ten finger prints. We would drive out to a small village and then check Iraqi IDs, scan retinas, fingerprint, take a picture and type in any known data. When I uploaded data later, I would see if there were a data match or a print or retina hit. If there were a hit, we went back to pick up the guilty. Fingerprints were primarily for bombs and went to the FBI; retina scans we used for camp workers. We loaded the top most wanted into the guard's retina scanners at choke points and in night raids. This was by far the most effective peacekeeping operation in Iraq.

My first BAT combat assignment was with the Third Recon.

The marines would hit a big town like Fallujah and kick everyone out. We then let everyone back in, but first they had to be entered in the BAT system. The locals loved it, because it kept known terrorists out. The troops loved it because of its speed; people could go through the line more quickly. Local sheiks, police, and leaders registered their AK-47 serial numbers and were allowed to carry weapons. You could not ever allow Iraqis to use the system, because they would trash all their enemies and other religions. It was respected, and they really wanted the system turned over to them. When I left in June 2009, the BAT people were trying to come up with a BAT light for the Iraqis. It seemed pointless to me, because the FBI and other departments would not want them to connect.

This was on display at Third Recon HQ.

The BAT team was very effective, there were no bombings on our watch.

Waiting for an available flight was part of daily life in a combat zone. Sometimes it was only a few hours, at other times it was a few days or more. If I was on a new install, I usually had priority, but you never knew. If my destination wasn't too far away, I preferred to go via a Humvee or MRAP(Mine Resistant Ambush Protected).

Transportation wasn't always ready when you were.

This is how I moved between camps in Iraq.

The V-22 Osprey was my favorite way to travel. It was like a twin-bladed helicopter that could lift straight up and hover. You could tilt the blades ninety degrees and take off and land like a twin-engine, fixed-wing aircraft, and it held plenty of cargo and had a drop back door like a C130. It rode like an amusement ride and gave you butterflies in your stomache.

My favorite mode of transportation during the war.

Ar Ramadi

I experienced my first real sandstorm of magnitude in Fallujah. The sand got on everything and messed up oiled guns, uncovered computers, and especially sweaty skin and eyes. I was reassigned when my Recon moved to al Assad, and I went to Ar Ramadi and the First Battalion Ninth Marines (the 1/9 Walking Dead Marines).

The 1/9 Walking Dead Marines, a very fine unit.

The 1/9 top sergeant issued me a tank/MRAP jump suit. It was quick and easy to dress and kept the sand out pretty well. He knew I'd be in the field with his troops. and I was part of his unit. The theater BAT leader was an ex-army master sergeant. He was small but in shape and had a good command presence. He was a motivating instructor and a great organizer. Just trying to keep up with him, I acquired many good habits, efficiencies, and the ability to use my "weapons" with purpose.

I was at last part of the solution; I still have
this jumpsuit and use it to cut grass

My field boss trained me hard and put in more time with me than with others. I was to be his replacement when he left on leave in mid- to late September. At first, we went to the different city gates and camp entrances; then to the exterior-supported firebases, FOBs, and choke points. Ramadi is between two lakes southwest of Baghdad. This is a high-traffic area and needs good security as it's a natural entrance to Baghdad from Jordan, Syria, and Saudi Arabia.

International was an outlying BAT station and FOB.

BAT is an all-encompassing system and tedious. There are eight pages to fill out—personal history, relatives, and current involvement. Then there are the inserted graphics: fingerprints, head picture, bar code, retina scan, and photographs of any weapons carried. Details from their Iraqi IDs showing tribe, current location, birth place and religious affiliation are also entered. A BAT station required an interpreter. We had to process the data to create a printed ID card like a credit-card-size driver's license. Once people are in the system, you can search where they have been and why they were stopped.

Teaching a class how to use the BAT equipment.

First I taught the system and how to use it, and then I moved on to the setup and troubleshooting. I'd taken sodas and water and gave them a fifteen-minute break. When they returned, I had taken apart all their equipment, and they had to reassemble it and take each other's data. Getting the printer to work was another phase that required focus, so I allowed them to make a picture card for their significant other. I told them to bring in a picture, and I would convert it for them. Or they could use their own pictures and put macho stuff on the card. This accomplished two things. First, it stimulated them into thinking about BAT, and second, it made sure they would return the next day. I made nice certificates for each person, which were included in their records. The officers liked it too, and BAT training became popular, not just a grind. Having a BAT certificate actually helped marines get promotions and the officers got high marks for mentoring troops.

The Camp Eagle BAT class; field classes away
from the base were in tighter quarters.

After training in Ar Ramadi and at various checkpoints, it was time to see the system in action and help the entire process. In-between, I swapped out laptops and uploaded and downloaded data from all the BAT sites. I gave instructions for the retina scanners to the line troops. If they got a hit on the hotlist, they verified it with the BAT people and then started incarceration procedures.

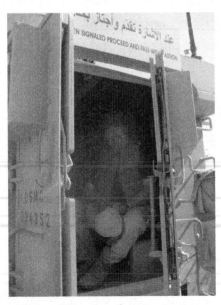

On a mission. We were always going somewhere.

By far, my boss and I caught the most terrorists and had the most new entries of people into the system. The army had more workers and troops than we did, but our guys saw the value and enthusiastically contributed to the mission. We had 100 percent coverage of our camp workers and transients. We scanned the retinas of many car and truck drivers and had choke points for pedestrian traffic, including facilities for burka-clad women. The mandatory age range for getting an ID and being fingerprinted was fourteen to sixty. Many volunteered because they wanted the ID. After age sixty, fingerprints are not very effective because the oil gives out. If you want to be a criminal, wait until retirement, and you'll have a better chance.

This next visit was strange. It was an interdepartmental visit to Blue Diamond, which comprised mostly Iraqi troops, but all the spooks and secret guys were buzzing around. They tried to blend in, but fooled nobody but themselves. Our mission was a "special" BAT for an Iraqi general and his staff. We put them all through the process and made sure their cards allowed them to carry weapons when in civilian attire.

Blue Diamond, the Iraqi and US troop checkpoint near Ar Ramadi.

With Iraqi staff officers and a reclining marine
corps officer (the intelligence liaison).

The general doted on a twelve-year-old boy, who was given whatever he wanted. His pistol was a nickel-plated, .32 caliber, and his uniform was impeccable. He "needed" an ID card with a weapon permit, per the general's special request. I complied and just shook my head, figuring if it's their country, then it's their rules. All the Iraqi brass paid the boy the greatest respect, and the Iraqi troops stayed away from him. They all knew his power over the general.

The Iraqi general was very concerned about his charge.

This twelve-year-old was the general's "boy," but he was not a relative.

War is all about positioning. You think about your defense, plan your offence, find your safe area, and set up your communications network, but you don't need to stress out. I believe posttraumatic stress disorder is self-imposed. If you hold your breath underwater, eventually something will give, and you will need to get to the surface. Humor was always my release. I identified with the movie *M*A*S*H** after I returned home from Vietnam. It was set during the Korean conflict but the overtones were of Vietnam. Humor can pull you through the worst things, and others will be encouraged and quickly follow. I have seen many "destroyed" people from my many combat experiences in the Middle East and Vietnam. The common thread is not stress—we all get that—but a lack of humor.

I also found a food I liked: dates. As I traveled around, I would pick a bunch of dates when they were dark yellow to brown. They were very sweet, and I can see how they got to be so popular.

Lots of sweets on a date tree

Our main weapon against the war on terror was a simple box. I've been in four combatant actions over almost forty-five years, and this by far was the safest and most friendly method of curtailing problems. I wish the BAT system had been available in Vietnam. As I uploaded collected data from all my BAT field laptops, I would download all the in-country collected data to date. My marine chokepoint guards always had the latest retina scans of 100,000 of the top sought-after terrorists.

One of my marines at ECP(Exterior Check Point), checking for the most wanted.

Printers were the toughest thing to maintain. I was constantly refurbishing them and cleaning them. If they were totaled, I took them down to the main repair center in al Assad. I would beg, borrow, and steal whatever I could to get my marines back up and running. We had a fairly good repair center in Ar Ramadi but not for printers.

To keep everything straight, my boss turned me into a cord Nazi. All my cords looked like small figure eights, neatly stacked on the shelf. It was good during night missions or equipment turnovers. We had more than a hundred BAT laptops, and twice a month they were updated. Some heavy usage posts were updated weekly. Things were rolling well despite our cramped storeroom and update table (we could do six at a time). Our guys were bringing in seven guys a week, three times the national Iraqi average. We were badging twice as many as any of the other sites and were the leaders across the board. The head of all BAT in Iraq was to visit to see what we were doing so right. My boss went on leave and left me in charge. Life was about to change.

I usually traveled in an MRAP between the fort and the ECPs or FOBs. But sometimes I was in an unarmored Humvee; it depended on what was available.

I was usually inside these well-armored vehicles. This was a smaller MRAP, used for intercity work.

The top enlisted marine was also the head of BAT in country, but he stayed in al Asad most of the time. He was dying to get in the field, so he came to visit the most successful post. He must have been bad luck for us. The day he arrived, one of the BAT ECPs west of town got hit. A careless guard allowed a guy to get past him, and he quickly ran in to my BAT guy's area and set himself off. He blew up all over everything, including an interpreter, took out the eye of one of my guys, and wounded the other one pretty badly. Both marines had a Medevac to Germany and eventually made it. The interpreter wasn't so lucky. My equipment was damaged pretty badly with brains, bone chips, blood, and bomb fragments. We closed down the ECP, which was mobile, not permanent, and I took all the equipment back. A marine from S-2 (security) took pictures, and I left.

The head of BAT was fascinated with the report and proceedings. He wanted souvenirs from the blast and took several pieces of equipment. He was not allowed the laptops, but I let him have the other stuff after he signed for it. The laptops were red-labeled "secret," and I had to return them with my report to the repair facility. Apparently the in-country boss didn't get out much and needed proof for his war stories. When I went to al Asad after this, he was always cooperative and got me serviced quickly. He knew I was in the shit more than most.

Not three days after my boss left, the 2/9 marines replaced the 1/9 marines. That meant massive work for me. BAT went on a lockdown after the suicide-bomber incident, but new guys were coming in and signing for the old units' equipment. The new guys also didn't have the skills, so my teaching went from twice a month to twice a week. Training, certificates, and field usage all had to be done. The new CO was impressed and quite enamored by my instruction and field operation skills. The old guys helped some too, before they exited out; the marines called it an RIP. They were on six-month tours only at that time. It was mid-October 2008, and I was a busy guy. I practically lived at the office, napping in my chair when possible. Marines came in at all times for equipment and instruction. Then the lockdown ended, so I had to get the ECPs and FOBs back up quickly. Those guys, I trained first.

Painted right over the 1/9 Walking Dead, the 2/9 Hell in a helmet.

I could teach a dozen in a class with six complete sets of equipment. Within a week, I had trained thirty-six, and with two per position, it was a start. I had the guards show the new 2/9 guys how to use the retina scans. On my one day off, I updated machines and did carpentry work that extended the office six feet by six feet. IT gave us a staging area away from the update desk. I took the old door off and moved it ninety degrees, and everything fit. It was still the same, but we picked up thirty-six square feet of space, about a third more than what we'd had.

I went out with the new 2/9 guys to check their progress. Jerry, an Iraqi interpreter, was on the mission as well. The day was hot for October, and the crowds of people were angry at delays. The new troops had itchy trigger fingers and were very nervous as the Iraqis processed through the ECP. I didn't want my troops to have an altercation so soon, so I took matters into my own hands. Many Iraqis speak some English; maybe a third can understand it. So I took Jerry out into the center of the crowd. I got up on a crate and spoke to them. Two-thirds were totally confused, so I told Jerry to stand next to me and repeat everything exactly as I said it.

I then said, "My name is Tom, and this is Jerry. We are going to give you the Tom and Jerry show, and I have a story about heaven and the pearly gates." Jerry repeated it, and they all stopped and were very quiet, as if I were an American priest. In Iraq, the cartoon *Tom and Jerry* is very popular and dubbed in Arabic.

Jerry; an interpreter has to be a great listener.

I told a little of my story, and then allowed Jerry to catch up. The marines were now also curious about the crazy, unarmed American geezer in the middle of the crowd.

I began, "A lawyer and a Catholic cardinal came up to the pearly gates to see Saint Peter. He took them for a visit around heaven and stopped at the most beautiful house with huge picture windows, right up close to God. He put the lawyer in the place with many lavish gifts and furnishings. Saint Peter then took the cardinal a couple of miles away to a basement with a leaky ceiling and one small window. The cardinal had to stand on his tiptoes and pull himself up to see outside. The cardinal said, 'What is wrong here? I have been a man of God my whole life, and you give me this damp basement while the common lawyer gets the beautiful penthouse place?' And Saint Peter said, 'That's true, but we have thousands of cardinals here, but that's the first lawyer.'"

It took a minute for the crowd to process the story, especially since Jerry had to repeat everything for the non-English speakers. Slowly the laughter began, and then it became a roar.

Jerry and I got off our crate and walked back to the marines, who were in a cheerful mood but still watchful. Jerry and I went back to the BAT booths, and the enrollment went much better for both sides. Even the marines were more interested in the process. Lawyers and religious figures are understood by all.

I had a mission to train at our farthest outpost. I needed three complete kits to swap out for their equipment. We were maybe a mile past a base called Duck Blind, and all hell broke loose. Explosions cause massive concussions and ring your bell. Ears don't work for a while, and you are somewhat stunned. We were stopped by an electronically detonated explosion under our MRAP from two 155 mm artillery warheads. It threw the vehicle in the air, destroyed the tires, bent and broke the rear axle, and completely blew of the transfer case and even the doors on the side.

Inside we were tossed around, but there were no IED fragments in our bodies. The bottom of an MRAP is like the bottom of a ship, and the blast angled up and out. I was alone and managed to open the back door and go to the rear vehicle. I sat down in the back of it. I heard chatter on the radio, and soon we were surrounded by Iraqi police and later a navy EOD(Explosives Operation Division) unit that checks out explosives and road incidents.

The chatter from Ar Ramadi S-2 was about the "PAX" in the middle vehicle. I was the PAX (short for passenger), and no one could find my body. I was confused but not that much. I could not call out; I could only listen. Everyone in security thought I'd been vaporized. The driver and gunner could not see my body and were partially dazed themselves. I could not alert them or get out of the vehicle with all the investigators looking for unexploded ordinance and reporting on damage. I was reported as dead to the new CO for 2/9.

The picture of my MRAP was taken back to Duck Blind after we were towed back, maybe three hours after the incident. When I get a close call, I am happy to have survived and about my good fortune. The marine behind me was the same; he played his air guitar. I gave the turret gunner some stateside beef jerky, and he came back from depression. I explained the happy side and joy of renewal as he chewed. In combat you focus on the moment. I am a fatalist, and if your number is up you can't hide.

I reported to S-2 and the CO that I hadn't been vaporized. My left shoulder had been bruised pretty good, but all was well. Knowing the military, they were relieved not to have to fill out all the paperwork in addition to still having their field trainer. It was a crazy day, and it was good to be back in Ar Ramadi. I went back to updating and training and returned to my previously interrupted field operation. My boss got back the second week in November. He saw the 1/9 had gone and the extended office, but when the

2/9 didn't recognize him and wanted me, that was hard on him. He was a good teacher and a good motivator. He had charisma and command presence but lacked mentoring skills.

*My MRAP was hit by two 155 mm howitzer shells,
buried in the road and set off electronically.*

My turret gunner was shook up because it was his third IED.

He sent me to the crossroads, an area beyond our normal range, but the people came to us for occasional help. I got there the day before Thanksgiving. These guys needed help and direction so I gave it. The classes relieved the boredom, and when they found out I could make cards for them or their girlfriends, everyone wanted in. This camp was platoon size, with maybe forty to fifty marines. I was the only civilian. Even the cooks were marines, but we did get one hot meal in the late afternoon. Otherwise it was MREs.

Thanksgiving was fun, and we somehow got rolled turkey, gravy, and mashed potatoes. The wine was just sparkling grape juice, but everyone was in a festive mood. After dinner we went outside in the sand, and they had built a bocce court. The sand was packed hard, and it had a canopy for daytime recreation. Four of us played, and they had real whiskey to drink. Apparently sending whiskey in mouthwash bottles was quite effective. I had a drink with them, and it burned good. Accommodations there were meager, but the comradery was great. I trained them and replaced damaged and out-of-date equipment and then returned to Ar Ramadi.

I don't know the politics, but I was ordered to pack my stuff and leave for Rawah. The 2/5 Marines were to be my next charge, along with a port of entry (POE) on the Syrian border and several FOBs. Rawah is at the top bend in the Euphrates River, and on the other side of the river is a small town called Anah. Interestingly had this area been retained, the current ISIS problem would have been stopped. This was the area through which they funneled their troops on the way to Baghdad via Ar Ramadi and Fallujah, both of which had fallen to ISIS by July 2014.

I flew from Ar Ramadi to al Assad to Rawah.

There was an ex-marine who was an unmotivated BAT guy and just marking time till he went home. I was not going to be that guy when I finished in six months. Pride and excellence sound corny, but they give you direction. Knowing that you make a difference and motivating others gives you power and respect. Commanding minimally, and leading by example is quite effective. I talked to the CO, and he got on board with training and mission. I'm sure it was his first command, and he was depressed after four months.

I saw the office; it was small but bigger than the original Ar Ramadi office. It leaked sand badly, but it did have A/C. My tent did not, but it was spacious. The tent also leaked sand. The furnace was at the other end of the tent where my BAT buddy slept. It was very cold at night in the desert, and we needed blankets. I didn't want to go to the latrine in the middle of the night, so I relieved myself in a quart container and emptied it in the morning.

My new home: a cheesy furnace and no A/C.

I got the current inventory spreadsheet and saw how badly it had been maintained. I still had a copy of the one from Ar Ramadi, so I renamed it and removed all the data. I entered all my coworker's data, but in red only. He asked, "Why red?" And I said, "It won't be black print until I have inspected each piece and verified its usefulness." Many of the pieces were not on hand but at the FOBs or POE. I had a mobile BAT recon unit with two machines that had not been updated for three months, and I trained and verified them first. They went to Anah and badged and checked the locals there. After they got their certificates, their attitudes changed. The CO took the unit with him wherever he went. They would badge local dignitaries and scan the retinas of all the attendees. He became a big supporter and helped me clean up the camp. Next on the agenda were the local camp BAT marines. We spent an hour just finding their equipment, and it had never been updated. I cleaned up the equipment and cases and trained the unit. As soon as they were done, I had them badge every camp worker. I gave them their certificates and a special award for the most improved unit in Iraq. All four made sure it was included in their personnel files.

It was mid-December, and the BAT guys wanted to go on leave. My guy went north to fill in for people on leave, so I had time to begin my "as is" inventory and validate all the equipment I could find. I told my far-off POE and FOBs to bring in their equipment for updating and get some training. Half responded, and I began with them. Most had equipment in need of repair, so I put it on a skid. I even had two spooks (CIA agents) come in with their equipment, which I repaired and updated. Interestingly, they had no data and had never badged anyone; they only checked on the data. They could however run the equipment very well. Too bad they were wasted in intelligence.

I finished the site inventory and maybe half of the FOBs, but I still needed to do the POE. The Syrian POE was the most important. I took a skid of broken BAT equipment on an Osprey to the al Asad repair depot. I filled out all the paperwork and copied my old buddy, the head of BAT, and of course my boss in Ramadi.

There was a replacement BAT guy coming in, but he was late. I think it was deliberate, because he didn't show up until after Christmas. He was not adventurous and did not ever take a vehicle anywhere. He took a chopper ride to Al-Qa'im once to meet me for equipment pickup, but when the ride back was in an MRAP, he balked. He waited there three days for a return helicopter ride. I had no use for him. He thought he was a server guy; he couldn't teach BAT or use it. He could upload and download data, so I kept him on that for a while.

I was slated for leave to spend time with my new wife from January 5 to 22. I had picked up some dry fungus, and it was bugging me so I tried a naval corpsman—there were no doctors—for temporary relief. He had cortisone cream, and that was it. I used it, and by that time the other guy was coming back from the north, so I knew it was my time for the border run. I took two operational BAT kits with me. Al Assad had called and said my order was ready, so this was the time to complete the mission before I left.

I went to the motor pool to catch a convoy that was heading west, and there were a couple of Abrams tanks there, so I took a Bob Hope picture, "Tanks for the Memories," to send my dad. I figured he would enjoy it because he had served in WWII and saw Bob Hope (as I had in Vietnam).

"Tanks for the Memories" in Rawah, Iraq

I arranged to have my FOBs meet me at Al-Qa'im, and I would train them together. I told them to bring all their equipment. Most of their stuff was in good order; it just was not connected properly. I assigned one guy to bring the laptops to Rawah and return them updated. I took from my kits whatever was missing and broken—usually the cameras and their cords—and made sure each site had an up-to-date laptop. They had only one day of classes, but they handled it well. I sent all their certificates to them before they went home in February. I think they were impressed that some old geezer civilian was out in the middle of nowhere teaching them.

I finally made it to the POE, where the marines had been trained, so I just had to check their update status, which took two days for one laptop. I put them on the same system as the FOBs and said, "Send one guy by plane or convoy with all the laptops but one and have him stay overnight, and he'll be ready the next day with everything." I answered questions on technique and about speeding things up. These guys processed a lot of people with just four BAT stations. I went on border patrol with two of them.

The Port Of Entry to Iraq from Syria.

My BAT marines, ready to start.

I walked over to the Syrian side, leaving my armed patrol, and no one said a thing. No challenge, just curiosity. A little girl broke the eerie quiet by crying; she was scared of me like I was the boogeyman. I got down on one knee and laughed, but she wasn't taking any chances and hid behind her mother's leg. The Syrian crowd loved it. I waved and walked back to my patrol over in Iraq amid all the Arabic buzzing. It was a very cool moment.

On the border between Iraq and Syria.

I worked with the marines all day and then went back to their camp. I looked at and inventoried all their equipment. There was a lot of broken equipment and a lot of missing parts. I knew what I had to do, so I stayed up all night and fully inventoried the broken and discarded stuff. I got their executive officer (XO) to sign off on it and left him a copy (they love that) and bundled it all up. I got a short flight but was cut at a FOB because it had already been booked with guys on leave. I talked to a gunny (E-7 marine), and he hooked me up with a convoy to al Assad. It took a little longer, maybe three hours, but I arrived safely with my marines.

I went over to the repair depot with all my paperwork done— the military was always amazed to see that—for the equipment

I was hauling. I got the other stuff on an Osprey heading to Rawah and told the unit to do the same when this equipment came through. I was one day early for my leave, so I called Rawah and told them I was leaving and that they should watch for the equipment. I took a C130 down to Kuwait and called my boss in ar Ramadi. I relaxed in Kuwait for a day and then headed out for Chicago.

When I arrived home, it was nice but very cold. I had that horrible fungus, and my left shoulder was still sore from the MRAP bombing incident. I used lots of lotions but could not get in to see a dermatologist until after my flight back to Iraq. My new wife was lovely and occupied by her ESL classes. She even had a couple of students to whom she taught voice and piano. It was very difficult to leave her again, but I had to finish the contract. I flew back after two weeks and got to Kuwait, but then I was stuck in TQ for three days. I finally found a marine and got an Osprey to drop me in Rawah. On the flight, I talked to some KBR guys who needed LAN hookups for their trailers. I said, "Okay, and can I get a trailer?" I moved out of the tent and reported the events to the XO, who was the second in command. I moved into the trailer and set the KBR guys up on the Internet, to their delight. I was in seventh heaven with a decent place, A/C, and my own bathroom and shower. The ex-marine BAT guy was going home and left immediately, and the other guy was still locked up in the office on the Internet and updating laptops. I asked about the equipment I'd sent before I left, and he said, "Yes, it's here."

It was down at the airfield, still on a skid. This guy just wanted to go home. He wasn't from my company or contract, so I called my boss for a chat. He decided to send this guy to the Jordan border—not the POE but the camp ten miles back, where they had a PX and served all three meals. I said okay and went about my inventory. I got everything done and upgraded the laptops. The guy got his orders, and the CO and XO called me in, explaining they were done and going stateside. It was February, and the RIP had begun. I stayed up all night and squared the inventory and the certificates for all the BAT marines in my area of responsibility. We had a ceremony, and all the certificates were placed in their personnel files. The officers were very proud of their troops. I went down to the motor pool and gave the convoy sergeant the certificates for the POE and Al-Qa'im.

Bradley tanks at Rawah, leaving for the Syrian POE.

The new group was the 1/5 Marines, who had been in Iraq two years before. I talked to the new CO. Interestingly; many of the troops were not citizens but guys from Columbia and similar countries who were looking to become citizens. He turned me over to the XO to get the training ASAP for the new troops and get the equipment sign over completed. KBR completed a new dining facility, and life was good. We now had three squares and no MREs except on missions. We got a PX with stuff in it to buy. They built a new all-purpose room, and I set up BAT training in it right away.

By the first of March, everyone was trained, certified, and properly inventoried. We were leading the country in badging.

The BAT teams were halted in April while they tried to sell the Iraqis a BAT light for themselves. I just kept the POE functioning and updated during the negotiations.

I felt betrayed due to all the work I'd put in. BAT was actually working, and the Iraqis loved it too. Politics confuses me because no one really knows the agenda. I've been in four wars—Vietnam, three years in Iraq, and time in Afghanistan, Kuwait, and Oman. I was fortunate to find my wife while I was in Oman, and I thought the BAT program would be great, but it turned out to be a marketing ploy to just sell a product. They loved what I did and wanted me to stay on for more money, but my shoulder and arm hurt, and it was time to move on. Later it turned out that I'd trashed my left rotator cuff; it required three pins, and my top-left bicep was disconnected and irreparable. I had two surgeries, but only the rotator cuff pins could be fixed the second time. I took early retirement at age sixty-two, three months after I left Camp Lejeune in June 2009.

I currently live in Hendersonville, North Carolina, with my wife and cat, Bazoonah, only a couple of miles from my parents.

The family back together.

About the Author

Tenacity has a triple bachelor's degree, a double master's degree, and many technical certifications from CISCO, Microsoft, and Novell. He and his wife Ivone have six children and four grandchildren in three different countries. They live in Hendersonville, North Carolina. This is Tenacity's second published book.

JUN 2016

WITHDRAWN

CPSIA information can be obtained
at www.ICGtesting.com
Printed in the USA
LVOW04s0911080516

487239LV00020B/743/P

9 781491 746813